TAILPIECES

By Deric Longden

TailPieces

1.

THE CARDIGAN CAT

I woke up in the usual way. A cat landed in the pit of my stomach and began pounding, up and down, up and down. 'Not there, Thermal,' I grunted. 'For God's sake.'

He turned round and worked his way up my

body, up towards my ribs. That's better.'

He moved on, ever upwards until he was standing with

one foot jammed against my Adam's apple, his white

furry forehead bopping hard against mine. 'Go away.'

He sat down on my chest and purred. I can do without Thermal first thing in the morning.

He was now lying flat out on my chest, doing his world famous impression of a very small hearth rug; his chin weighing heavily upon my chin, and with each one of his four paws splayed out as though he had been recently filleted and placed there as a practical joke.

One of his whiskers poked itself right up my left nostril and began to investigate its inner regions. I snorted and the whisker panicked, flirting smartly back in to line amongst its colleagues where it trembled slightly as it told tales of its great adventure.

The bedroom door creaked open and out of the corner of my eye I watched as Aileen crept silently in to the room. My wife is registered blind and has to feel her way around. She stopped in her tracks as her hand brushed against something black and hairy lying stretched out on the cane chair.

She knelt down and began to tell the cardigan off in no uncertain manner.

'You're not supposed to be in here, you know.'

The cardigan took not the slightest notice of her. It was a one hundred per-cent woollen cardigan with raglan sleeves and large horn buttons and it wasn't used to being spoken to like that.

'You dribble all over the cushion.'

That cardigan had never dribbled in its life. I could swear to it. I had worn it man and boy for the past ten years, first with pride and then with a growing defiance as it began to look its age. Now I wore it in secret in the garden, whenever the evenings grew chill. But in all that time I had never known it to dribble, not even once.

'Come on Arthur - get off.'

The cardigan never moved a muscle. I think it was in shock. The thought of being mistaken for a cat was bad enough. To be mistaken for the scruffiest, most disreputable cat in the neighbourhood would form the basis of an impassioned court case at the very least.

Granted it was going a bit thin at the elbows and the horn button with the bit missing was hanging on by a thread and a prayer. But to be mistaken for Arthur - well, the shame of it.

'It's no good you pretending to be asleep.'

Aileen knelt by the chair so that she could get a good close look at him with her fingertips. Before she picked him up she needed to sort out which was the head and which was the tail. When Arthur arrived on our doorstep he had two broken back legs and a broken tail and we have to handle him with great care.

She patted the cardigan, gently at first, but then with a mounting suspicion as she stroked its woolly back.

It was when she got her finger caught in that little tab that you hang it up on the back of the door with, that the truth finally dawned. Arthur doesn't have a little tab that you hang him up on the back of the door with and so she rose quickly to her feet, casting an embarrassed glance over her shoulder in case anyone had been watching. She hates being caught out like that.

I hadn't seen a thing. I'd been fast asleep throughout the entire incident and so had Thermal, and he'd had his back to the action anyway. So she heaved a small sigh of relief as she slung the indignant cardigan over the back of the chair and then came over to wake me up.

She sat on the edge of the bed and stroked my hairy chest with a puzzled frown.

'It's Thermal,' I told her, and so she scratched the back of his neck and Thermal purred even louder.

It's hardly worth while getting up, I thought. Nothing interesting ever happens in our house.

2.

HEY, IT'S LUNCHTIME.

There were only ten minutes to go until lunch. South

Africa were batting. Cork was on at one end and

Malcolm was due to bowl from the other. They both play

for Derbyshire and I am a Derbyshire man myself.

'I won't be a minute.'

Thermal was sitting on the hearth rug staring up at me.

'Look into my eyes.'

'I told you. In a minute.'

He moved closer and parked his little bum in between

my feet. The he switched his stare up on to main beam

and the vertical hold on my concentration began to

waver.

'I'm watching this.'

But only just. I missed that delivery and it was almost

lbw.

'You are beginning to feel drowsy.'

'Stop it. I shan't tell you again.'

There was a movement behind me - a pincer

movement. First Tigger sprang lightly up on to left arm

of my chair and fixed me with her pale blue gaze.

'Look into my eyes.'

Thermal shifted his position slightly.

'It's all right - I've done that bit already.'

Then Arthur shambled round the back of the chair and sat side by side with Thermal on the rug.

'Has anybody told him what time it is?'

Thermal nodded and then his stomach rumbled right on cue. I don't know how he does that - he's had it down to a fine art ever since he was a kitten.

They do this to me every lunchtime. Usually we are all in the kitchen. Aileen and I will be having a light snack and then in come the animals, one by one.

They sort themselves out in to a line, shortest on the left, tallest on the right and then, in unison, they sit down and stare meaningfully at the fridge door.

Frink the kitten hasn't quite got the hang of it yet. She usually arrives late, takes one look at the others, and then with her front paws buttoned up tightly together, she sits down and stares meaningfully through that glass bubble on the front of the washing machine.

'Get that kid out of here - she's ruining everything.'

But today I was determined to stay with the cricket. It's not as though I could just nip in to the kitchen, open up a couple of tins of Whiskas and then slap the stuff in to four bowls.

It takes time. Frink has to be fed up on the working surface, her saucer tucked away out of sight behind the kettle so that Thermal can't get at it. Arthur likes his milk first and only when he's finished the last drop will he tackle the speciality of the house.

Tigger is on a diet and she must have heard somewhere that you shouldn't take liquids with your meal. She hardly eats anything at all. I think she's anorexic. I have to get her all worked up by making a great show of half-opening the tin and then letting her have a sniff through the severed lid.

'You'll like this Tigger. Egon Ronay swears by it. He mentioned it in the *1994 Good Food Guide.* He said it was a very good year - worth laying down.'

By the time I've finished I could almost eat it myself and Tigger is jumping up and down with excitement. But after the merest perfunctory nibble she realises it's just the same old recipe as before and she saunters off with her head in the air.

At least I don't have to worry about Thermal. He doesn't eat - he Hoovers. I watch him chomping away, fascinated, hoping he might stop before he gets down to the lino tiles.

But today I was going to be firm with them. They could wait until the cricket was over. Come on - concentrate. Pay no attention to them.

Three little bodies sat absolutely still as their big round eyes drilled in to my subconscious. I can handle this - I'm bigger than they are.

Then the kitten bounded in. She jumped straight up on to my lap and plonked her bottom down, her eyes boring straight in to mine.

Oh my God - she's got the hang of it. The others must have sent her away on a course. I wondered why she'd been coming home so late these past few weeks and now I knew - night school. *Staring for beginners: How to win meals and influence people.*

I gave in. Three pairs of liquid eyes were all I could handle. The extra pupil was just too much for me.

3.

IT'S ALL DONE WITH TUNA.

The electrician put his head around my study door. He doesn't talk to me much as a rule. I once took a three-pin plug apart and asked him what seemed to me to be a very reasonable question.

"How long have they been making the earth wires green and white?"

He lives, eats and drinks three-pin plugs and he knew right there and then that we had nothing in common and so he now conducts all his business through Aileen.

"When you come and get your cat - it's going to kill itself." He had the floorboards up in the back bedroom and so we trooped upstairs together.

"Which one is it?"

"That daft one."

That didn't help much - I have four of those, but as it happened it turned out to be Thermal.

"I can't stand cats," he frowned I find it rather difficult to explain and so I always make some idiotic remark or other.

"You've got to admire anything that can jump ten times its own height."

He wasn't convinced. "If it touches them bare wires it'll break its own record." I put my head down through the hole in the floorboards and spoke very firmly. "Come on

Thermal, let's have you out of there."

I should have known better. There was a pounding of paws as a very independent cat raced upside down, right under the floorboards, over to the far corner of the room. "If that was a dog, it would do as it was told."

It was no good telling him that I didn't want something that came running the moment I called. I wanted my animals to live alongside me - not in my pocket. All the same I am sure I could have found a couple of Salisbury's small Atlantic prawns in the fridge if a certain cat had chosen that moment to come and join us up on deck.

There was a shout from downstairs. "Mr Longden - can you come and sort this out for me?"

It was the man who was putting air vents in the kitchen cabinets - we've had a bit of damp. "It's that blessed kitten of yours," he said. "It's gone up the chimney."

I put my head through the hole in what used to be a fireplace. "Come on Frink, let's have you out of there." I never learn. I tried everything but he just sat there, up on the flue - I could see his paws. And then I remembered the advice my mother once gave me.

"Try making a noise like a mackerel."

Well I couldn't remember ever having heard a mackerel. David Attenborough was my sole contact with the wider world of nature at the time and even he drew the line at dolphins and whales. "Here let me show you," she had said impatiently, grabbing a can of mackerel fillets from the cupboard and a tin opener from the drawer. She opened the can very slowly, just by the cat flap and in no time at all she had a cat sitting beside her, drooling on the kitchen floor.

I tried it now with a tin of tuna. "Did you know a cat has twenty muscles in each ear?" I asked the builder, but he wasn't impressed. "I can't stand cats," he frowned.

It worked a treat. Both Thermal and Frink appeared within seconds and I congratulated myself on my sense of economy. I had opened the same tin twice, the top for Frink and the bottom for Thermal, thus making the most out of our only tin of tuna. Aileen wasn't so pleased - it was a tin of tuna with mayonnaise and she was going to have it for her lunch.

Still it was a small price to pay and the electrician was done and off in no time. The builder was going to be with us for a little while longer and so I put my head round the kitchen door to see if he wanted a cup of tea with his snap.

Thermal was sitting by the breadbin, eating a piece of

ham that the builder had plucked from one of his
sandwiches.

"Catch."

Tigger had a slice all to herself under the kitchen table
and the kitten was sitting on his knee, being fed gently
by hand. Arthur would be furious - he hates missing a
party.

The builder saw me standing in the doorway and the
frown came down like a shutter.

"I can't stand cats," he said.

4.

LITTER TRAY BLUES.

"Well that's the winter over and good riddance. It's not
the snow that gets me down, or the ice that brings me
tumbling down - it's the cat litter that has me down in
the dumps for months on end as I heave the great sacks
up from the pet shop in town.

Arthur costs me a fortune. His litter tray is about the size
of Wembley stadium and still he only manages a direct

hit once in every three attempts.

He's never quite got the hang of it. As long as he has two front paws buried up to the knuckle in cat litter he assumes that his back end must be in there as well.

I don't like to say anything. I wouldn't want to embarrass him. He likes to keep himself to himself and he wouldn't know where to put himself if I were to make an example of him in front of the others.

In fact, he can barely manage to clamber in over the side these days. It's those back legs of his, he just can't get the leverage.

I suppose I could fix a little pair of swing doors for him up at one end, but they don't seem to sell them in Petals and Paws.

He did once make a suggestion, but I've never taken him up on it. "Why don't you spread some on the carpet, right round the edges, then it won't matter if I have an accident every now and then."

So it's a great relief now that he's able to pop outside again. At least when he performs in the garden you can be pretty sure he won't miss.

I hardly need to bother with Tigger. She has the exclusive use of a huge meat tray that I found round the back of the butchers, but I only have to freshen it up every now and then. She's only used it on the one occasion when she drank something she shouldn't have done from a bucket in a neighbour's garden and her legs wouldn't work for a while.

She was mortified. I carried her from the settee where she was recuperating and as gently as I could, sat her down on the tray.

"Don't look then".

She tried to cover it up when she had finished but she was too weak to manage and so I did it for her.

"This is very good of you."

"Don't mention it."

And I think in that moment we bonded in a manner that very few cats and their owners have ever done, before or since.

Thermal and Frink have their trays side by side in the cellar. There, after a long and tiring day, they can tot up the days triumphs and sort out their tactics for the following morning.

Having the trays butted up close together was especially useful when Frink first arrived as a kitten and was still trying to get the hang of it. She only had to peep over the fence to witness a master in action.

And then the winter came and the garden froze over and

Thermal began to see the sense in it. Now it's God help any passing feline who might assume that this was common land. He'd have their guts for garters.

Frink's tray is the smallest of the lot. Once it was pan of a decorating kit, the sort of tray you use in tandem with a paint roller, but it does have one great advantage. She's the only one of four with a deep end and a shallow end.

I keep telling myself that it's going to be different next year. But after the mess Yorkshire Water have made of things these past twelve months, I will probably have to go and buy another litter tray. A big one that Aileen and I can share. Somehow I can't see her going out in to the garden.

5.

WARMING TO GLOBAL

I couldn't understand where the cats had got to. I had a

pan of rabbit simmering on the stove and they must

have caught wind of it by now. I opened the back door.

That should bring them scampering home, even if

there were off chasing cars on the M62.

But it didn't. It brought Global, the world's roundest

kitten, chugging in like a tug boat through the open

back door. I have no idea where he comes from.

Word has it that he lives in a pub somewhere not far

away, but that could be just a rumour brought about

because he looks like a beer-belly on legs.

When I think about it, he's been a kitten for an awfully

long time. I must ask him about it sometime.

'What do you do for a living, Global?'

'I'm the only professional kitten in Huddersfield.'

He appears every now and then, rolling remorselessly

along, with his head down, studying the ground

immediately in front of him, acknowledging neither

man nor cat nor Mercedes Benz.

Cars don't exist in Global's world. He ploughs across

the road and it's up to them to either stop or weave their

way around him.

Dogs are even less in evidence. The smaller variety jump to one side when they see him coming and the larger ones, who have more to lose by a show of cowardice, simply stand stock still and are walked under.

There is something about him that defies description, so don't ask me to me tell you what it is. But I can vouch for the fact that when Global walks in to your kitchen you feed him.

Food is all that matters to him. He doesn't get excited about it, he's a professional after all. He just eats.

I found a half-empty tin of tuna with garlic and herbs in the fridge and I spooned it out in to a saucer.

Global immediately began his demolition job, pushing the saucer round the kitchen floor in front of him as he ate.

He has been genetically engineered for eating out of saucers. Walking as he does, with his head never more that half-inch above ground level, he is perfectly positioned to take advantage of even the most unexpected saucer the moment he comes across it.

The saucer did one complete circuit of the kitchen table, arriving back at the starting point as clean as a whistle. And for once Global had some sort of an expression on his face.

He couldn't quite work it out. There was no doubt that the herbs went well enough with the tuna, and the garlic had come as a pleasant surprise, but that certainly wasn't the aroma that had assailed his nostrils as he walked in through the back door.

His antennae whirred just the once and immediately took him over towards the cooker where he stood like a little pot pig, his head pressed hard against the glass door, his eyes firmly fixed on the nearest lino tile.

I'd had enough. Entertaining Global is like having the Mafia round for tea. I picked him up and turned him round.

I don't think he's real. As my hands slid underneath his fat little belly I half expected to find a couple of Duracell batteries, tucked away in a small compartment.

He doesn't like being picked up. Not that he says anything or does anything about it. He doesn't communicate in the normal way. He employs a brand of body language that is still as a duck pond and yet thick with unspoken expletives.

'That was very rude, Global.'

'Up yours.'

The last time I held anything this shape in my hands I was playing football, standing on the touchline waiting to take a throw in.

I planted him on the back step and gave his bottom a push. He set off like a small tank, across the courtyard and down the path, without so much as a by your leave.

If he thought he had found a soft touch in me then he had better think again. I had enough on my plate without catering for a cat who thought of me as just another rusty link in his food chain.

But as I went in to answer the phone I knew full well that the next time he came calling I would find him something or other, I always did. He has an aura about him. I could smell it now and so I gave the kitchen a quick burst with the air freshener before I picked up the receiver.

6.

ALL CLEANED UP

It seems only yesterday that I was the proud owner of a curious collection of comatose cats. A secondary wave of winter weather sent them in to late hibernation and they sprawled about all over the place.

For a week or so I kept my accounts, my calculator and a spare cat in my desk drawer. As I pulled it open there would be Thermal, blinking at the light with just the one eye, in no mood to waste his energy by fraternising with the staff. He'd only had nine hours sleep since he tumbled out of bed that morning and if he didn't get his head down soon he would be too tired to sleep when it came round to bedtime later that night.

Tigger could have got a little closer to the Valor living flame if she'd crawled right inside the gas fire, but that was too much like hard work and so she settled for pressing her bum up against the brass surround. Frink the kitten spent hours fast asleep in what we once called the fruit bowl. I remember the golden days when it was stuffed full of apples and oranges, with the odd grape thrown in for good measure.

But Frink decided she liked it in there and took up vacant possession and from that moment on it was constantly fur-lined in off-white and ginger and every five minutes or so it rattled to an earth shattering snore.

I was just about fed up with them. I could excuse Arthur. He hasn't been very well for some time now and the vet decided to put him on a course of vitamin injections, but he's a tough old soul.

Every morning he would take his early constitutional out to the dustbin and back again. Then last thing at night he would slope off and hide and wait for me to come looking for him.

Since he always hides under the bed in the little back bedroom it never takes me very long to find him, but the exercise does us good. His heart pounds a little faster as he sees my feet coming towards him from under the counterpane and then I have to carry what amounts to a small cart-horse down two flights of stairs.

I began to get quite worried. Every other cat in the neighbourhood seemed to be living life to the full. They were out and about, climbing trees and spraying bushes and digging up small bedding plants by the dozen, while my motley crew couldn't even muster up enough energy to have a good scratch.

Then last Monday morning the cleaning ladies from hell arrived and the spell was broken. I didn't even know they were coming. Aileen arranged it.

My study door burst open and in they came, three of them, with dusters and buckets and a vacuum cleaner that looked like one of those things the council use for sucking out drains.

They wore leather belts with holsters and they fired Pledge from the hip. They had sprayed Frink twice and polished her once before they even realised she was in residence. Tigger got caught by stray burst of Ajax liquid as she made for the door and if she's no better next week she's going for counselling.

I plucked Thermal from the drawer and we made a break for it, down to the lounge on the ground floor where we shut ourselves in. I had grabbed Arthur on the way down. He was suffering from shock and smelled faintly of Pine disinfectant.

'It suits you, Arthur.'

'Thank you.'

No matter where we went the cleaners sought us out and by the time they had finished we were nervous wrecks. One by one the cats drifted out through the back door, hesitating for a moment on the step as though they had forgotten what outside was all about.

'It's big, isn't it?'

'If we stick together we shall be all right.'

And now I can't get them back in. They have rediscovered the joys of outdoor pursuits. Such as jumping on next door's rabbit, pulling up the primulas and the last one up to the guttering's a cissy.

I miss them. The house is so fresh and clean it makes your eyes water, but there's something comforting about having a cat on tap in your desk drawer. You can't stroke a calculator and a bowl of fruit doesn't purr in its sleep. Never mind - soon be autumn once again. Driving rain and howling winds, freezing fog and instant cats. What a lovely thought.

7.

ANOTHER ONE JOINS THE GANG

I don't know what made me do it. He was probably the

toughest looking cat I have ever laid eyes upon, and I've

seen some belters in my time. My mother once had a cat

called Horace. He was short of one ear and one nostril

when he first planted his bottom on my mother's back

doorstep and she wondered whether she should take in

or not.

"Somebody must be missing him."

I tried to imagine the sort of person who could possibly be missing a cat like Horace and failed miserably. My mother went to have a word with him.

"I think he's a bit deaf in his left ear."

"He hasn't got a left ear."

"He's got a lovely smile though."

And he had. He also had great dignity, which is more than you could say for the cat who had just planted his broad bottom on my back doorstep. It could have been mistaken for a rather dishevelled hyena.

My first thought was to lock all the doors and draw the curtains and pretend that Aileen and I had taken the cats and gone off to Cornwall for a fortnight.

We had plenty of food in the freezer and a huge stock of cat litter in the cellar. We had enough down there to sandblast the Town Hall twice over. We could hide until he had gone away and want for nothing.

And then I had another look at him. He was a big cat, there was no doubt about that. You could have thrown a saddle over him and entered him for the 2.30 at Chepstow.

But a second glance told me that all might not be well with him. His coat hung loosely about his body, like a cape; as though he had tossed it carelessly over his shoulders on the way out of the house and not even bothered to do up the buttons.

As he settled down to a crouch, he took it in stages. First he thought about it for a while and then seemed to be explaining to his limbs exactly what was required of them.

It was as though his legs had never done this before. As though they couldn't remember whether they were supposed to bend forwards or backwards and it was some time before they managed to arrange themselves neatly, tucked away underneath him and out of sight.

I once saw a wildlife programme in which David Attenborough followed the last days of a tired old lion. He was too weary to catch his prey unless it came out of the bushes with its hands up. I kept shouting at the television.

"For God's sake, David. Stop whispering and feed the damn thing." But he didn't and the lion died a long slow death. I couldn't have that happening on my own doorstep so opened a large tin of Whiskas and poured half a bottle of milk into a soup bowl.

As I pushed the door open it occurred to me that perhaps I should have brought a chair along with me. "Easy now. Down boy. Back - baaack"

He looked larger than ever out here. Even with his

bottom still glued to the stone step he was much taller

than any two of mine put together. "There you are, boy.

Try that." He rose and lumbered towards me. Despite

his obvious problems he was still an awesome creature.

He had little tufts of hair sticking out of his ears. Did we

have wild lynx in this country?

Then Tigger strolled out through the open door and

made straight for the two dishes. First she gave the milk

a proprietorial lick and then she had a quick nibble at the

steak and kidney.

I feared for her life. He'll tear her limb from limb, I

thought. But he just plonked himself down by the side of

her and waited patiently until she had completed the

tests. She stood back.

"I think you'll enjoy that."

"Sure you've finished?"

"Please. Be my guest."

And with that he tucked in, the plate travelling along in front of him and across the courtyard. He came back for the milk and mopped it up with a tongue the size of a loofah. Tigger smiled indolently.

"Let me show you the accommodation."

And with that she escorted him down the cellar steps and showed him the large cane chair with the Dunlopilla cushion.

"I think you'll find it's very comfortable."

He hopped aboard and settled down. I think I've acquired another cat. It's easy when you know how.

8.

CATS IN A FLAP.

I counted them out and I counted them in. An hour

earlier I had watched as four furry bottoms disappeared

through the cat flap, and now, as I finished tidying up

the cellar, I watched as our heroes returned, one by one.

Frink is always bursting to tell me of her great

adventure. Her eyeballs on stalks and her hair standing

to attention.

"You didn't."

 "I did."

"You could have been killed."

 "I know I could."

 "You're a very brave kitten."

"I know I am."

Tigger bustled in after her, like a mother hen. "You want to have a word with that kitten."

"She's been telling me all about it."

"She could have been killed."

Tigger gave Frink a quick clip round the earhole. She must have really overstepped the mark this time.

Arthur was the next to arrive. He doesn't actually use the cat flap as a cat flap any more. Old age and arthritis have stiffened his back legs and so he just pops his head through the hole and asks me if I would be kind enough to open the door. I am thinking of buying him a mobile phone.

Thermal treats the cat flap as though it were the last fence at Hickstead. With his front paws elegantly outstretched and his head tucked deep in to his chest, he sails through the little sheet of plastic to a burst of imaginary applause. Then he sets off on a lap of honour.

I remember my mother trying to teach her cat Whisky how to use the cat flap. For the best part of a year she sat him beside her on the kitchen floor whilst she banged her head against the back door. He would stare at her in total bewilderment.

"Go on. Show me again."

Then one day he got the hang of it. He was outside and it started snowing. The cat flap seemed the lesser of two evils.

I say he got the hang of it and he did, but only in his own fashion. He came in backwards. First his bum appeared through the hole and then two back legs and a tail. He waited, wondering what he should do next. My mother had only ever taught him the theory of cat flap technology, she had never actually passed through the door herself.

And so he took his fate in his own two paws and reversed a little further in to the kitchen. And as he did so the flap crashed down on the back of his neck and his two ears pinged against the underside.

From that day on he always came in and went out backwards, always pausing for the inevitable thump on the back of the neck. The cat flap gave him a new found sense of freedom and a permanent headache.

One day Whisky was sitting on the back door mat,

staring in through the open door.

"Come on Whisky. Come on boy."

He just sat there, gazing at me as though I were from another planet. My Mother bustled in to the kitchen and I pointed him out to her.

"He won't come in."

She sighed. Did she have to do everything for her idiot son? "Of course he won't, not with the door open."

She slammed the door shut and within seconds the flap started to rise and two back legs and a furry bum began to ease themselves in to the kitchen.

For my cats the cellar is a halfway house. All the other outside doors are over a hundred years old and it would be a crime to punch holes in them and so the cats congregate down there, waiting for me to escort them onwards and upwards.

I've done what I can to make their waiting room as comfortable as possible. Two cat baskets and a couple of easy chairs are grouped around the boiler and there's a piano in one corner if they fancy a sing song.

Frink often sleeps in the cellar, in a converted tea-cosy. She goes in through the handle hole and peeps out through the spout hole. It could have been made for her, but she's growing fast. The other morning she came upstairs and she was wearing it. She looked like an upholstered tortoise.

As the lost tribe and I passed through the hallway on our way up to the canteen, the front door bell sounded and Aileen stood there looking flustered.

"I forgot my key."

I think we need a bigger cat flap.

9.

So, you're back.

I turned the key and pushed open the front door. Then I

pushed Aileen in through the narrow gap and followed

on behind with the suitcases.

'Why do I always have to go in first?'

'They wouldn't hit a woman.'

'They might.'

They certainly looked as though they had been thinking

about it. Thermal wore a glower that hung somewhere down around his knees and Frink the kitten sat by his side, trying to match her hero, frown for frown.

Fortunately she hasn't quite got the hang of it yet and so she just sat there, glaring at us like a gerbil with acid indigestion.

Arthur wore a black scowl that threaded itself right the way across his forehead and then disappeared round the back of his neck. There was a sort of sneer on his lips, the sort of sneer that comes only with watching too many Humphrey Bogart movies. I must get him away from that television and out into the open air once in a while.

Tigger looked very hurt. How could we possibly have gone away for a whole week and left her like that? She'd had some dirty tricks played on her in her time, but this one took the biscuit I bent down to stroke her head and as always her timing was perfect. She bobbed under my hand and then turned and stalked away leaving me squatting there on my hands and knees, reaching out in to thin air. Thermal looked on in envy.

'I wish I'd thought of that.'

It was time to show them who was boss and all I managed to do was to show them that it certainly wasn't me.

'Come on now. Bridie looks after you very well.'

But apparently Bridie had slipped up on more than one occasion. First of all she had given Thermal his breakfast without rubbing his tummy first and everyone knows how rubbing your tummy aids the digestion. And then she had shut the back door on him - just because he didn't know whether he wanted to go out or not.

'She knows I like to sit and think about it for an hour or so.'

Arthur complained about the way the food had been served.

'She left it out all day. It had a crust on top. You could have trotted a mouse on my beef and kidney Whiskas.'

Frink thought very hard, which is unusual for her.

'And she trod on my ping-pong ball.'

'No she didn't - it's over there. I can see it.'

'Well - she nearly did.'

It's always the same. It's the price you pay for a few days away. I can handle the three musketeers.

'I've brought you some prawns.'

'What sort of prawns?'

'The ones you like - the big ones.'

Thermal's knees buckle at this point. He loves prawns. He dreams at night of being out on the lone prairie, where herds of wild prawn graze in the long grass. He stalks them silently for a while and then with just a shuffle of his backside and one almighty bound he brings down the dominant male, dragging it back to his lair where he shares his booty with an adoring wife and cubs.

'Really big ones?'

'Enormous.'

'Oh, all right then.'

The other two will forgive me if Thermal does. Arthur because a rumbling stomach takes precedence over just about everything else and Frink because she has no idea what on earth is going on.

But Tigger takes her time. There are more important

things in life than giant prawns, thank you very much.

Loyalty for instance. How can she trust me ever again.

For the next twenty-four hours she will avoid me. Her

body sprawled out in the most uncomfortable places she

can find, her baleful eyes switched instantly to accusing

mode the moment I walk by.

Then, just as I am beginning to think that this time it's

forever, there will be a rustling under the duvet and a

warm body will wriggle in by my side.

'Tigger?'

She purrs like a twenty-ton truck when she's hungry.

So we'll go and sit in the kitchen in the early hours. Me

with a cup of tea and a cigarette, Tigger with the plateful

of prawns I put one side for her.

She'll manage to force them down and then jump up on

my lap.

'Friends again?'

And she will butt me and fall asleep on my knee and my sins will be forgiven. After all - I'm only human, aren't I?

10.

AN EVENING IN.

What more could a man want? Curled up on the settee with a beautiful woman, a bottle of rich red wine and a good film on the telly.

Well in our house there is always the added bonus of four sprawling cats, three of them with heads as heavy as lead and a small ginger and white kitten with the sharpest elbows north of Watford.

Arthur always stayed firmly anchored to the hearthrug. He had his image to think of. As a kitten his one ambition had been to play rugby league for St Helen's and there was no way he was going to become a lap cat overnight. Then one cold winter's evening he looked up and saw the rest of the family all snuggled up together and he must have felt left out of it. He landed on my knee like a sack of potatoes and he's been the first one on duty ever since.

He's actually a two lap cat. He never learned the noble art of curling up and so I always get the end that polishes off the Whiskas and Aileen finishes up with the end that strongly resembles a flu brush.

The other three have had to improvise and so they have

become experts in draping themselves around necks, shoulders, thighs and any other bit that sticks out. Aileen suffers in that direction more than I do.

We've got used to it by now. We can sit through a whole movie, not daring to move in case a comatose cat might answer the call of gravity and slide down towards the carpet.

Not that they ever would. Their braking system works even when they are out like a light. Four sets of specially sharpened claws dig in and hang on until either the blood runs red or the cat wakes up.

Fortunately my leg will have been fast asleep along with the cats for the past hour and so it doesn't hurt all that much. I've got used to it now. What I can't cope with is when they decide to play *stiffening up.*

Stiffening up is a game played between consenting cats and gullible adults. The cats, who up until now have been snoring gently in unison, will suddenly wake up as one moggie and swivel their heads sharply, stiffen up and stare in unison at the door. They must have heard something - have they seen anything?

I switch on every light in the hall and then on the stairs, brandishing a vicious looking milk pan in my right hand shouting, 'Is there anybody there?' in a deep masculine voice, very loudly so that any intruder will have a sporting chance of being halfway up the M62 before I appear on the scene.

It always seems to happen just as Charlotte Rampling is about to take her clothes off and by the time I return to the television she's got most of them back on again. It's so frustrating.

There never is anybody there. The cats seem to have a warped sense of humour, but Aileen gets her own back on them.

All four of them sit for hours on the window sill in her office, staring out at the side road and the garden path, waiting to bang on the glass if a passing sparrow happens to set as much as one foot on our wall.

Aileen sits beside them, swinging her legs and staring aimlessly out of the window. Then, all of a sudden, she swivels her head sharply, stiffens up at stares long and hard at nothing in particular on the garden path. The cats go rigid.

'What?'

Aileen is locked in a trance, eyes wild and staring.

'Have you seen something?'

The cats, now looking as though they have been recently starched, try desperately to pick out whatever it is she is looking at.

'Where is it?'

Aileen packs it in just before the twitch in Arthur's eye is in danger of becoming a permanent affliction. You would think it might teach the cats a lesson, but it never does - it just makes us feel that little bit better.

But only for a little while. In fact Tigger has just paused in mid furk, her left hind leg stuck high in the air, wavering dangerously just inches from the bulb in my desk lamp. She's staring at my office door - she must have heard something.

So if you'll excuse me I had better go and investigate.

Could be burglars. Now where did I put that milk pan...?

11.

A CAT IN LOVE.

Thermal has fallen in love. It's a platonic affair. A visit to the vet, one wet Wednesday morning some years ago, made sure there was never any chance of it being anything else. But it's the real thing for all that - or despite the lack of all that, whichever way you want to look at it.

Marlene is a pretty little thing. Her eyes are limpid pools

and she sits with her front paws buttoned up together, as a lady should. She's a chintz like Tigger, black, white and ginger, and she wears it well.

I think Tigger's jealous. Under normal circumstances her love knows no bounds. She spends most of her nights combing the park for drop-outs and cat-nip addicts. Then she brings them home, two or three at a time. They troop in through the garden gate, strung out in a line behind this very small Mother Theresa in the hairiest of hair-shirts. You can smell the meths on their breath as they settle themselves down for a good night's sleep in the cellar.

She once brought home the most amazing trio. They could manage only eleven legs, four and a half ears and two tails between the three of them. And the one with a tail missing had never been anywhere near the Isle of Man in his life.

No matter how ill-mannered, or however badly it smells - if it looks as though it might possibly be a cat, then Tigger will love it and cherish it and give it a home.

Within a week of arriving here herself she adopted a fully grown rabbit in the mistaken belief that it was a long-eared pussy cat with a very bad limp.

His name was Flopsy Arrowsmith and he lived in a hutch at the end of a garden three doors down. The Arrowsmiths were worried at first. Especially at the sight of their rabbit trotting off down the pavement in the company of Tigger and Thermal, who had been brought along to ride shotgun.

But eventually they accepted the situation and then when

they went off to Majorca for a fortnight they asked Tigger to babysit for them. She got the best of the deal. Thermal and I had to look after Neville, the Arrowsmiths' parakeet, whose main hobbies turned out to be dive-bombing cats and whitewashing the furniture.

If she had been around at the time of St Francis, Tigger would have sat at his right hand and been in charge of administration and really bad cases.

But she can't stand Marlene at any price.

'What on earth's wrong with her?'

'She's nothing but a tart.'

'I quite like her.'

'Well you're a man, aren't you?'

And after yesterday's events I'm beginning to think Tigger might have a point after all.

Aileen and I were watching television. Arthur was fast asleep on top of the radiator. We wanted to turn up the heating but we would have roasted him alive and so we huddled closer together instead and used Tigger and Frink as body warmers.

The room was aglow with the warmth of contented domestic bliss until the moment Thermal arrived on the scene with his lady friend.

First of all she began to chat up Arthur.

'My. You're a big boy, aren't you?'

Then she jumped up on my lap and walked up my chest, totally ignoring the fact that she had had to tread on Frink's head to do so. She fluttered her eyelids at me and butted my cheek.

'Let's get rid of the others, shall we?'

Her poise slipped slightly when Frink belted her one for treading on her head, but she rallied strongly and was well ahead on points until Tigger belted her for belting Frink.

Over by the radiator Thermal was telling Arthur off for chatting up his girlfriend and Arthur was telling Thermal that he wouldn't touch her with a bargepole.

Aileen had had enough.

'Stop it now', she yelled. 'You're behaving like animals.'

Well they couldn't really argue with that. I tucked Marlene under my right arm and firmly propelled her out through the front door while Thermal went off to have a sulk in the back bedroom.

We haven't seen her since and life seems to be back to normal now.

Peace on the hearthrug and goodwill to all cats except

Marlene appears to be the order of the day.

It's amazing how one bad apple can upset the cart.

My mother put it perfectly many years ago. 'She's all fur

coat and no knickers.'

How my mother knew about Marlene I shall never know.

12.

SEASONS GREETINGS

There are times when you have to be firm, even at

Christmas. I looked her straight in the eye and spoke my

mind,

'Good will to all men, that's what it says. It doesn't say

anything about stray cats.'

Tigger drew herself up to her full height. Eleven and a half inches on a good hair day.

'But he's nowhere else to go.'

'Of course he hasn't . Have you taken a good look at him lately?'

Even Tigger had to suppress a slight shudder as she glanced over to where the scruffy old stray lay slouched on the wet cobbles, slurping disgustingly as he was re-decorating his nether regions with a tongue the size of a yard brush.

'There's a nice side to him.'

I couldn't help wondering which side that would be. It certainly wasn't the side he was pointing at me. Of all the courtyards in the all the world, why did he have to limp in to mine?

'He's got fleas.'

'We all get the odd flea from time to time.'

Not like this cat they didn't. This cat had fleas like the Pied Piper had mice. Thousands of them. Generation after generation must have grown up in those furry depths, snug as a bug in a rug. And what with jobs being so hard to get these days the kids would still be living at home with their parents. Laying about drinking all day, or zipping around on their skateboards and playing loud music at nights.

'Sorry Tigger. Not this time.'

But cats never take no for an answer. Dogs understand the meaning of the word - and so do cats. They think it means: "Go on then - seeing as it's you."

For the next few days she worked on me with all the skill of a spin-doctor at a party conference. Every time I looked out of a window, there would be the moth eaten old cat, with Tigger sitting gently by his side, willing me to change my mind. But I was determined not to give in, never in a million years.

'Go on then - seeing as it's you.'

I can be very firm when I want to be.

My first move had to be to gain his confidence, but Tigger had already had a word with him.

'Don't worry. He's as soft as grease.'

The old cat let me pat him on the head and then allowed me to stroke his gritty back. Have to get rid of those fleas, I thought. It must be standing room only in there.

My cats will have nothing to do with the spray can. They

make a break for it the minute I open the cupboard door. But this old chap must have been as deaf as a post. He just stood there and took it - gradually disappearing in a mist of fine powder.

I could only imagine what must be going on under that matted jacket of his. Thousands of fleas running up and down the decks, lifeboats being lowered over the side, muffled shouts of "Women and children first." I felt like a murderer, but it had to done.

Then I combed him and back-combed him. And he seemed to grow to about twice his original size. He looked a treat - albeit a rather self conscious treat. All I had to do now was to see to his split ends and ask him if he needed anything for the weekend.

I don't think the other cats recognised him when he

trotted in through the back door. Thermal for once went all macho and thought for a moment about protecting his territory.

Then he thought again. You don't muck about with a cat that looks as though it is about four-foot across, and anyway, it was Christmas after all.

The old stray liked it here. You could tell. First he sprayed the back door and then he sprayed the front. Then he set about spraying everything in between.

He just couldn't understand why he was sitting out in the courtyard again, minutes after being welcomed in through the back door. As far as he was concerned he hadn't put a foot wrong. Perhaps he should have brought a bunch flowers for Aileen that must be it.

He's settled down in the cellar for the time being, until I

can get the message across, and I'm trying not to feel too guilty about it. After all, Jesus spent his first Christmas in a stable and He didn't have central heating and net curtains.

Perhaps the three wise men will sort him out.

13.

A ROUND WITH TYSON.

'He's a nice cat,' she said. 'Once you get to know him.'

She called him Tyson and off-hand I couldn't think of a

more appropriate name. Hitler would have suited him. Or

maybe Mussolini, taking into account his considerable

bulk. But since he was black as coal, Tyson would do

very nicely indeed.

Getting to know him was going to be a problem. She put him down on the carpet and he immediately began to sharpen his claws on the coffee table. He stropped his huge paws up and down the antique leg as a barber might sharpen a cut- throat razor. The name Sweeny Todd sprang to mind.

I smiled at him. My winning smile. The one where the corners of my eyes crinkle up like little Venetian blinds and you can tell at a glance that I am a very kind person who might have walked straight out of a Disney film.

'And who do you think you're looking at?'

I tried my stern look. The one that once made Clint Eastwood hand over his gun that night after I missed the bus and had to walk all the way home from the cinema.

Clint had apologised profusely, even grovelled a little, as we passed Mr Patel's Rent a Video and Pizza Parlour and while I was on a high I went in and asked Mr Patel if I could rent a pizza for the weekend. He had absolutely no idea what I was on about. And neither had Tyson. My stern look had no effect whatsoever. I thought he might roll over on his back and offer to hand over his claws, but instead he jumped up on to the coffee table and strolled over towards me.

'Go on, punk. Make my day.'

I had offered to look after him sight unseen, for a long weekend was how she had put it, and I was about to find out just how long a long weekend can be.

'Perhaps he would be happier staying at your house. Then I could pop in and feed him over there.'

'He'd wreck the place. He can't stand his own company.'

So we arranged that he would come over here and wreck

my house instead and I told the cats not to do anything to upset him.

'He looks like a cat, but he's really a Pit Bull Terrier in disguise.'

Tigger said he was probably just misunderstood and she would appeal to his better nature. Thermal said he would thump him if he tried anything on, but then when Tyson arrived he took one look at him and decided to fly south for the winter. Or rather he hid under the bed in the back bedroom for the entire weekend.

'I think I'll take my meals up here if you don't mind.'

Tigger did have a quick look for his better nature but he didn't seem to have brought it with him and she soon decided that what he needed was professional help, complete with straight jacket, tranquillisers and a long pole.

'He has to go in the cellar.' I told Aileen.

It's quite nice down there. Carpeted throughout, with the central heating boiler in a prime position and a piano up against the far wall. He would want for nothing.

'Stick him in my study.' said Aileen. 'I'll sort him out.'

He went straight up the curtains like Chris Bonnington and sat on the pelmet, breathing fire and brimstone. I couldn't leave her alone with him - a blind woman and the cat from hell?

'Push off,' she said. 'And leave us alone.'

For the next couple of hours I tried to work, but my imagination was in overdrive. From across the landing came the unmistakable crashing and banging of an animal in the thrall of mad-cat disease, punctuated by unnerving periods of silence that seemed even louder still.

Eventually the silence took over pole position and I crept across to Aileen's study and eased open the door, wondering what I might find. Perhaps just a shoe and the odd torn remnant of dress fabric - plus a hunk of black fur here and there to show that she had put up a brave fight.

Aileen lay fast asleep on the settee and Tyson lay stretched out by the side of her, his front paws resting protectively on her hip and one of his wicked yellow eyes resting itself on me.

'Push off,' it said. *'And leave us alone.'*

He stayed in her study for the rest of the weekend, as good as gold, and I asked her how she'd done it.

'I just ignored him.'

'How did you know that would work?'

'Well, it always has with you.'

14.

NEXT PLEASE!

There were two other cats there when we arrived at the

surgery, both of them tucked up behind the bars of their

portable cat baskets. An enormous Alsatian sat by the side

of a little old lady who could have passed for either its

owner or its lunch.

Over by the fireplace there sprawled a small round dog

who seemed to have been put together by a committee and something even more compact rustled inside a flat cardboard box that shook ominously on the knee of a teenager who wore a purple anorak and a vacant expression.

I couldn't think what he could possibly have in a box so square and flat. Perhaps it was some sort of a snake, all curled up like a Danish pastry. I shuddered at the thought and Thermal dug his claws in the back of my neck and held on for dear life.

He lay wrapped around my shoulders, his hot breath rifling my left ear while one of his back legs poked around in the other one on the right-hand side. I leaned forward a little and shuffled him up a notch.

'Thank you very much.'

'My pleasure.'

He hadn't been feeling too well for most of the week. He had slumped in front of the fire all day, just taking the odd trip over to his litter tray and back again whenever the urge came upon him. But since that was all he ever did during the first few months of the year I hadn't noticed anything was wrong until he politely declined the offer of a prawn-cocktail crisp.

I knew then that something was amiss. He has been known to lie and cheat for a prawn-cocktail crisp. I wouldn't put it past him to maim and kill. And so within the hour we were taking our turn in the waiting room.

I should have known earlier. I suspect he had a temperature and if he hadn't, then I had. It can get awfully hot when you have a cat wrapped round the back of your neck. He whispered in my ear.

'She won't use that glass thingy. Will she?'

'She might have to.'

'You won't look, will you.'

'Of course not.'

He gets most embarrassed when they take his temperature. Sitting there with a thermometer sticking out from under your tongue is one thing, having it sticking out from under your tail is another matter altogether.

The Alsatian whined piteously and the smaller dog looked across with undisguised contempt. Wish he wouldn't do that. Not with all these cats around. Lets us down, it does.

The young man in the anorak was in and out of the consulting room in a flash. He still had the vacant expression but he had left his box behind with the vet and I wondered what she would be able to do for a sick snake. I wouldn't even know where to stick the thermometer.

The nurse consulted her card index and called in the next patient.

'Major Bowden.'

I waited for the Alsatian to make a move but it was the smaller dog who rose to his feet He marched in, not waiting for his owner, back straight as a ramrod and his head held high. All that army training I suppose.

Thermal and I were the last to be called and the vet gave him a thorough going over.

'Don't look.'

'I won't.'

Then she gave him an injection and he was very brave. Then she felt him all over and he enjoyed that. She's known him since he was a kitten and they get on very well.

I was waiting for Thermal to get dressed when a fully grown rabbit burst in to the consulting room, from the private office round the back. He did an about turn when he saw us, skidded on the lino, and his feet went from under him. Then he crashed in to the skirting board and I bent down and picked him up while he was still stunned.

'Perhaps he was frightened by the snake.'

The vet looked bemused.

'The one in the box.'

Thermal didn't talk to me all the way home. I think he was ashamed of me. But how was I to know that the vet had been out in the country all day? How was I to know she that hadn't had time to eat? How was I to know she'd ordered a pizza?

`You won't tell Aileen, will you?'

But Thermal just licked his sore bum and snorted. And after all I've done for him.

15

THAT SMUG CAT NEXT DOOR.

I try not to wash the car too often. It weakens them. I washed it last August and I'm sure it almost caught the flu. It was shivering and shaking all the way down to London.

If the big end goes I can always take it to the garage, but what if it catches pneumonia?

But on Wednesday Aileen was speaking at a dinner. She took one look at the car and said if I didn't wash it she was going on the bus, and so Wednesday morning saw me out on the drive with a bucket of soapy water and a chamois leather in my hand.

Chris was out there, scrubbing his Volvo. He had just about finished when his cat Roly leapt off the garage and landed on the car, leaving a skidmark on the roof and several wet pawprints on the bonnet.

What made the incident so memorable was that at the time the cat had a very dead and very stiff woodpecker clamped in his mouth.

Now if Chris's wife had jumped off the garage roof and landed on his newly cleaned car Chris would have killed her, even is she hadn't had a stiff woodpecker in her mouth.

But Roly gets away with murder. He has an instinct for

the rarer creatures of the countryside. He specializes in rabbits that are twice his size and he once caught a squirrel.

Admittedly it had arthritis and an artificial hip, but Roly is a vicious little devil and there are times when I fear for the cows as they chew their cud at the bottom of his garden.

To Chris's credit he didn't like to see his cat with a dead woodpecker. Chris likes his woodpeckers with some get up and go and this woodpecker's get up and go had got up and gone. He hurled his sponge at the cat and Roly went hell or leather for the cat flap in the kitchen door.

Have you have ever tried to go through a cat flap with a dead woodpecker stuck in your mouth? No of course you haven't - it's a stupid question. But if ever you do, make sure that the woodpecker isn't suffering from anything as drastic as rigour mortis.

Roly hit the flap at about ninety miles an hour. His front paws went through first and then the top of his head and then he came to a sudden and unexpected halt as the stiff woodpecker jammed itself solid either side of the woodwork.

The effect, as they used to say in the beer adverts, was shattering. If it had been a *Tom and Jerry* cartoon, he would have turned to smile at us and then all his teeth would have dropped out.

As it was he turned with a glazed expression and sank in to a heap on the floor. I thought my *God,* that's must be the first time a cat has been killed by a dead woodpecker. But Roly is made of sterner stuff. After a saucer of milk and a snort of catnip he was up and about and sitting on the highly polished bonnet of my car.

'Get off.'

He glared at me and padded all over my paintwork. Then he sat down and tried to outstare me, which if I'm honest doesn't take all that much doing. Slowly I began to inch the car out of the drive.

I have never driven a Rolls Royce, but I imagine that the winged figurehead must be rather like a cat with big ears sitting on your bonnet. At the bottom of the road I touched the brakes gently and Roly began a controlled slide and made a mighty leap for the safety of the pavement.

When I returned he was stalking a donkey in the field.

'You have to be firm with them', I told Aileen.

The next morning I opened the front door and as I did the acrid smell of ammonia filled the air. It had been sprayed as though with a hosepipe.

I set about with the disinfectant and as I scrubbed away I could feel eyes boring in to the back of my head. Chris and his infernal cat were grinning at me over the wall.

I knew then, as I looked in to that wicked face, who was responsible. That curling lip, that evil sneer, those cold smirking eyes - smug with satisfaction.

But then again – I suppose it could have been the cat.

16.

THERMAL'S GRAVY TRAIN.

I have been trying to catch Thermal at it for some time now. Yesterday I caught him redhanded. He denied it of course.

'I never.'

'Oh yes you did, I saw you.'

'You mean you were spying on me?'

'I was keeping an eye open.'

He thought it was despicable. If we couldn't trust one another, he said, what future did we have as a family unit?

But I was ready for him.

'And what future do we have if you go licking the gravy off everyone else's Whiskas?'

'I was testing it.'

'It doesn't need testing.'

'Oh, so we're an expert on cat food now, are we?'

He stormed off in a huff and Thermal in a huff is something to behold. He beat the living daylights out of Aileen's fireside rug and then belted several small ornaments off the mantelpiece, before setting about a poor innocent little toilet roll who had never hurt anyone in his life.

Tigger took it all in her stride, but Mills and Boon looked on in amazement. They have only been with us for a couple of weeks. Two rather scruffy strays who arrived in the cellar from nowhere and are still somewhat shell shocked.

After what must have been several months of self catering they still can't believe that they have hit upon a place where the food is delivered twice daily, and milk and nibbles are always on tap.

They probably wouldn't recognise gravy if it jumped up and bit them. In fact I know they wouldn't because they are hardly likely to have seen any. Somewhere along the food chain, Thermal has been licking it off.

I suppose it's my fault really. The security has been

rather lax. Thermal works as my literary assistant and so he is by my side throughout the working day.

He sits on my desk and is in charge of paper clips. He keeps them on their toes. If it wasn't for him, he says, they would just lie there in that little plastic thing doing absolutely nothing all day long. So he keeps them on the move and sees to it that they hardly have a minute to themselves. By five o'clock they aren't fit for anything but a good long nap.

And so Thermal knows my routine at feeding time. I lay out the twin-section bowls in the kitchen, all colour coded and sparkling clean. Then I dish up the Whiskas, pour a little milk in the second compartment and go off looking for my customers. That way it's all ready for them to tuck straight in when they arrive and the delay helps take the chill off the milk.

By the time I have the bowls all topped up they look almost good enough to eat and I take a great pride in my presentation. I once stuck a sprig of parsley on top just for fun, but Thermal almost choked to death and so I haven't tried it since.

I couldn't help noticing however that the glaze seemed to disappear very quickly. One minute the bowl of Whiskas looked as though somebody had recently been at it with a varnish brush and the next it was just a pile of uninteresting cubes, leaning against each other, bored out of their skulls.

At first I thought the gravy must be sinking like a stone, but then I put two and two together. I went as though to round up the raggle taggle army and then doubled back and watched as Thermal moved along the line of bowls, his tongue flashing in and out like a little pink spatula on speed.

Thermal's huff took him off across the road to where Liz would spoil him and tell him what a clever boy he was. In the meantime the paperclips were able to have a nice long lie in and they were just about to turn over, having had a good long stretch, when the prodigal returned and told me all about it.

Apparently he's worried about BSE. His theory is that the answer lies in the gravy. BSE has a bitter taste to it he says, and he can tell it straight off. His dad once worked with the caretaker at the Technical College and so he knows all about these things.

As senior cat he decided it was his task to sample each

meal and maybe lay down his life for the others. Isn't that wonderful? I had tears in my eyes by the time he had finished. He's an example to us all.

17.

ALL WOKED UP!

The television chefs have it all too easy. The ingredients to hand, in bite-sized bowls, minced by minions beforehand and laid out in the correct order. Not a pot to wash afterwards and not a single cat in sight.

They ought to try it in our house. A studio audience would be a doddle after cooking for years in the presence of four critical cats.

'Oh hell. He's getting the wok out again.'

Aileen bought me the wok for Christmas, complete with stainless steel cleaver and hardwood board. For my birthday she bought me an asparagus steamer. She really knows how to spoil a guy.

The cats hate to see the wok come creeping out of the cupboard. They know that the bottle of soy sauce is likely to follow hard on its heels and they can't stand soy sauce at any price.

'He'll ruin those prawns.'

They can't stand the sizzling and spitting either. What was wrong with the old fashioned beef and two veg? Done in the oven as God intended. You knew where you were in the old days.

Then they could sit, two of them either side of our chairs, looking up appealingly, catching odd bits of rogue beef in mid air. Every now and then a lump of coarse horseradish would slip through the security net and have them flat on their backs, coughing fit for their lungs to burst. But the offending morsel could always be rinsed under the tap and then you could hardly tell the difference.

Best of all were the scrapings from the meat dish, together with the leftovers. That was really living. But have you ever tried licking out a wok? No wonder those Siamese cats always look as though they've just eaten something that didn't agree with them.

But they brightened up considerably when they saw the avocado I had bought to go with the prawns.

'He doesn't muck about with them.'

I had to muck about with this one. It was hard as a rock. It had lain there in the fruit bowl for over a week now and still you could have used it as a baseball.

The cats moved in for a closer look. All except Tigger who wouldn't dream of doing anything so vulgar. She stayed aloof, sitting with her paws buttoned up tight together, over by the stove in the corner.

The avocado took the edge off my cleaver as I sliced it in half and then I had the job of removing the stone. It was as though it had been set in concrete. I stuck a knife in and fiddled around. But this one was going to need major surgery.

I dug deep and twisted hard and the stone shot out like a bullet. It flew across the kitchen, clipped the ceiling light and then dropped like - well like an avocado stone, I suppose.

Tigger was minding her own business, filing that claw on her left paw, the one that's always given her trouble ever since she was a kitten.

She was just slipping the claw back into its sheath when the avocado stone descended from the heavens and smashed down on top of her head.

The effect, as they say in the advert, was shattering. Her legs folded up underneath her and she fell over and got up, only to fall over again and then she staggered about on the kitchen tiles like a heifer in an abattoir.

I picked her up and her eyes rolled and she seemed to pass out. I didn't know what to do. The kiss of life perhaps?

'Where am I?'

She played the scene to perfection. It was just like an old movie. She even gave a polite cough to suggest that there might possibly be a hint of consumption.

I took her up to my office together with half a dozen prawns and you would be amazed at the healing properties a half a dozen prawns possess. They ought to be on prescription.

After a while she curled up on my chair and fell fast asleep. It's not really allowed during the day, but there were special circumstances and Tigger is not one to let a special circumstance go by without giving it her full attention.

The noise from downstairs was horrendous as three small cats belted an avocado stone around four skirting boards.

If ever an avocado stone paid for its sins - this one did.

So did the prawns. They'd had the lot. Now where did I put that cleaver?

18.

WHEN I SAY LOOK...

I hoisted Thermal up on my shoulder and pointed him in the general direction of the squirrel. It had just done a handstand on the garden wall and was about to attempt a triple somersault with half twist and rupture.

'Can you see him? Over on the wall, by the gate.'

Thermal shifted himself slightly and then peered deep

into my left ear.

'*I think you've got a bit of wax.*'

'Never mind that.'

I plucked him off my shoulder and held him out to dry in front of me.

'There. Straight ahead of you.'

The squirrel was by now performing selected excerpts from *Riverdance* on a low lying branch, just to the left of the ornamental chimney pot. He was a natural, but Thermal missed him. He was busily examining a small imperfection in the window-sill.

'*You want to touch that up. It'll spread like wildfire.*'

'Never mind that.'

I pressed his body up against the window pane and his nose went a funny shape and spread all over the glass.

'I can't breathe.'

'Sorry. I just wanted you to see this. There, look. He's on the stone mushroom.'

The squirrel had chosen the mushroom as the perfect place to take a standing ovation. He bowed to all four corners of the garden and then, somewhat disappointed that no one had thought to throw flowers, he turned and made his way back to the park.

Thermal in the meantime had screwed his head upside down and was having a good look at the underside of the pelmet.

'You missed it.'

'Missed what?'

You can't point a cat at anything. They just don't want to know. They think you are trying something on.

Thermal's neck takes on all the qualities of a bendy toy if I so much as attempt to draw his attention to anything remotely interesting and his eyes cross over one another until they meet up round the back of his neck.

It's so disappointing. I can't really enjoy anything thoroughly unless I share the moment with someone else. If there's a good film on the television and I am in on my own I want to run out and drag people in off the street.

'Here come and look at this. You'll love it.'

The other cats are just as bad. Tigger comes running to fetch me the moment she spots anything that takes her fancy, such as a spider on the hearth rug.

'Come and watch this. I'm going to duff him up and I want a witness in case he sues.'

They also play a game called stiffening up. It's a game played between consenting cats and gullible human beings. Aileen and I will be watching television with the cats spread at regular intervals along the hearthrug - a tranquil scene of domestic bliss.

Then, as one, the cats will swivel their heads sharply, stiffen up and stare in unison at the door. They must have heard something - have they seen anything?

I switch on the lights, shouting, 'Is there anybody there?' in a deep masculine voice so that any intruder will have a sporting chance of being halfway up the M62 before I arrive on the scene.

There never is anybody there - it's just the cat's warped sense of humour, but Aileen gets her own back on them.

Tigger stares out of Aileen's window, waiting to bang on the glass if a passing sparrow happens to set as much as one foot on our wall.

Aileen sits beside her and then, all of a sudden, she will swivel her head sharply, stiffen up and stare at nothing on the garden path. The cat goes rigid,

'What?'

Aileen is locked in a trance, eyes wild and staring.

'Have you seen something?'

The cat, now looking as though it has been recently starched, tries desperately to pick out whatever it is she's looking at.

'Where is it?'

Aileen packs it in just before the twitch in Tigger's eye is in danger of becoming a permanent affliction. You would think it might teach the cats a lesson, but it never does - it just makes us feel that little bit better.

But I must be off now, the squirrel's decided to make a come back. I wonder where Thermal is?'

'Thermal come and look at this. No, not there - over there by the roses. Can you see him? Yes I know they are very pretty curtains, but that's not what I'm on about. Look at the squirrel for God's sake.'

Next time round I'm going to get a glove puppet.

19.

CATFLAP FATIGUE.

I gave the cat flap a squirt of WD40. That's about as technical as I get. The cat flap is on its last legs and no wonder. It handles more traffic than the turnstiles at Wembley stadium.

There was a time when it stood proudly at the cutting edge of modem technology, an electronic wonder that opened and shut whenever the cats' collars gave it the password.

Nowadays it just hangs on in there, wincing every time a furry little head bops it in the stomach. Denton started the rot. He's a ginger tom from down the road, built like a brick outhouse and as thick as two short planks. He has spent his entire life at the cutting edge of total ignorance. And yet it didn't take him long to come up with a solution. He would sit outside, waiting for one of our cats to come bounding out through the cat flap and then he would catch it with one paw, before it could swing too.

Once in he would mop up enough food for a whole army. His only problem was that he couldn't get out, not until one of the residents came bounding back in again and that's how I caught him. Waiting by the cellar door with his paw cocked ready and his overloaded stomach slung close to the ground.

So our new found technology was turned from white hot down to stone cold sober in next to no time at all. Collars went mysteriously missing and the cat flap swung open to all comers. And a good thing too. We began to welcome a string of no hopers, an endless procession of beaten down losers in search of a square meal and a bed for the night.

Arthur was the first to arrive. He was cowering in the park after some idiot had thrown a bucket of creosote over him. Tigger found him and brought him home. Burnt and broken, but with his dignity still intact.

Two hundred and seventy one pounds worth of vet's fees later he decided to repay me by moving in permanently, and he was worth every penny.

Others come and go. Little Chap appears once a fortnight and I can't make him out. He's the mildest gentlest, most civilised of cats and yet he chooses to live a life full of drugs, booze and women.

So every two weeks or so we dry him out, feed him up and let him sleep for twenty four hours. Then he's off out with the lads again. I keep telling him he needs a hobby - he says he's got one.

The cat flap is in the cellar, because I wasn't about to cut holes in solid oak doors that are over a hundred years old, and it couldn't have worked out better.

The central heating boiler stokes the place up to gas mark 37 and there's a perfectly good carpet that didn't quite match the new three piece suite.

Light pours in through a window set halfway up the cellar steps, illuminating a vast array of extras designed to maximise feline potential. For the musically inclined a piano stands in one corner, and my sturdy old Amstrad sits on the workbench, should they wish to hone their literary skills.

They have an old microwave oven which still works in ten second bursts, long enough for a medium-rare mouse, and there's a television set that is quite capable of receiving BBC 2 if the wind is in the right direction and nobody moves.

Best of all - there's a vast collection of cat baskets, gathered from some of the finest second-hand shops in West Yorkshire, each of them fitted with a plumped up cushion to ensure maximum creature comfort.

And yet every morning, when I go down to feed this shifting population, I find them fast asleep on the piano, under the piano, in the sink, up on the top shelf, literally on a bed of nails. Anywhere but in the custom built accommodation.

This morning I found Little Chap dozing in a cardboard box full of polystyrene pebbles. He must have been wet through when he came in last night and the pebbles are stuck all over him. He looks like Larry the Lamb on a bad hair day.

I've sheared him twice already, but the pebbles are clinging on for dear life and he's getting fed up with it. He thinks I'm trying to pull the wool over his eyes.

Think I'll give him a squirt of WD40.

20.

COLLIE – CAT.

At first I thought it was a dog. Aileen thought the house

was on fire. I leapt up from the settee and dashed out of

the room.

'There's a big black and white Collie coming up the

path.'

At three o'clock in the afternoon as well. Siesta time,

when slumbering cats are at their most vulnerable.

I took the stairs two at a time, which was a big mistake.

There are thirteen of them and going down the last one

two at a time was just asking for trouble. I rolled over twice and hit my head on the occasional table with the Queen Anne legs. It's a wonder Queen Anne ever managed to stand up if she had legs like that. It toppled over and fell on top of me.

I had watched the Collie come prancing up the path on close circuit television. We have two cameras, one trained on the front path and another on the courtyard round the back and we watch them for hours. We could look out of the window and see the same thing but it isn't anywhere near as much fun.

For a start the cats have no idea that big brother is watching them and so they leave their cuddly-toy image behind them and behave like proper cats.

Take Tigger for instance. Inside the house she is a sweet

little creature, butter wouldn't melt in her mouth. She drapes herself round the back of my neck as I work at my desk, murmuring gentle words of encouragement. She could purr for England.

If Thermal takes her favourite chair then she wouldn't dream of disturbing him.

'No please. He looks so comfortable.'

But once outside the house she stands no nonsense from anyone. One look from Tigger will reduce the fiercest of strays to a quivering heap and sooner or later Thermal will get a short sharp clip round the earhole for daring to sit in her chair.

Even so, pound for pound, she wouldn't stand much chance with a fully grown dog. And neither would the others by the look of them.

Little Chap was lying fast asleep on his back. He always sleeps like that, with his mouth wide open and all four legs stuck up in the air. Today he had chosen the low wall by the catmint and was about to fall off at any moment.

Thermal was curled up, fast asleep, on the ornamental stone mushroom, doing his world famous impression of a Danish pastry. Only Tigger was wide awake and her ears reported for sentry duty the moment they heard footsteps coming up the path.

Collies are nice dogs, I told myself. Gentle souls who devote their whole lives to social work with sheep. At worst he might round up my cats and drive them off.

But what if he was a rogue Collie? A Collie who had had it up to here with sheep and was about to take his revenge on society, starting with my cats.

It didn't bear thinking about and I was just beginning to panic when the biggest black and white cat I've seen in years came ambling round the corner.

If Postman Pat's black and white cat had been the size of this one he could have done his round in half the time, sidesaddle.

It was enormous animal with a pointy nose and it was making straight for Tigger.

'Sorry I'm late.'

'That's quite all right. Have you met the others?'

He hadn't and so first she introduced him to Thermal who was very pleased to see him, and then to Little Chap who had just fallen off the wall and was checking his private bits and pieces to see if they were all there.

The newcomer seemed an amiable old soul and although

he was twice the size of your average cat, much of his bulk comprised of a black and white coat that he had borrowed for the occasion.

It certainly hadn't been made to measure. It fitted where it touched and his tail stood to attention, as though he were towing a cart behind him, on which stood a small Christmas tree.

He's been with us a week now and we've all fallen in love with him. I advertised him in the local paper as a gentle giant but nobody came forward and that's fine with me.

He hasn't taken his coat off yet, but I do hope he's stopping.

21.

HURRICANE WILLIAM.

We are still getting used to having William about the place. It's not just the size of him, it's his enthusiasm that keeps us awake at nights. We are taking it in turns to have a heart attack.

William doesn't enter a room - he takes it by surprise. He bursts in, having started his run somewhere along the M62. The door flies open and suddenly a huge black and white blur is part of the furniture, fixtures and fittings, scattering papers and sleeping cats and turning hearthrugs into instant hump-backed bridges.

After he had been with us for a week or so I took him to see the vet, to have him checked out. We were shown in to an antiseptic consulting room, white as snow with just a single well scrubbed table and a freshly sluiced tile floor.

But the moment I carried William in through the door the room instantly became incredibly untidy. As Mrs Roger turned him upside down to examine his undercarriage I could see her glancing around, thinking, I must have this place done out - it's a disgrace.

It's not that William is a scruffy cat. His white bits are as white as you can get and his black bits glisten like newly polished ebony, but his hair is as fine as silk and the slightest breeze keeps it constantly on the move so that even when he's fast asleep he appears to be either on his way back from somewhere or just about to leave.

The other cats don't know what to make of him. Thermal is a sweet natured little soul - he gets it from me. And he's done his best to make William welcome. The moment he arrived he took him straight upstairs to show him his rapidly expanding collection of cat-biscuits through the ages and William was most impressed. Then he took him to have a look at the fridge in the kitchen but unfortunately it was shut. Early closing day or something.

He showed him what fun it is to sit on the draining board and catch drips with your paw. William thought that was terrific - he has paws the size of buckets and it came to him easily.

He even let him to have a go with his ping-pong ball. William found it dozing round the back of the settee, having a quiet five minutes - which is something it hasn't been allowed to do since.

The trouble was that, without really knowing it, we had settled down in to a cosy routine. You know the sort of thing. Thermal likes to have a stroll round the estate just before midnight, smelling the flowers and hurling abuse at itinerant slugs.

Tigger waits for him on the back door step and then the two of them go and sit on Mr Barrett's wall and stare at his Alsatian until it barks and Mr Barrett comes out and tells it if it doesn't shut up it's going back to the PDSA. Innocent little pleasures like that.

Then they have their supper and settle down for the night, Thermal on the fax machine and Tigger on the top shelf of the airing cupboard.

Our days had been pre-programmed and set to run on automatic and then William arrived and the cold wind of change blew through every corner of the house.

Coffee tables hurled themselves to the floor the moment they saw him coming. Ornaments jumped to their death rather than meet him face to face and he developed the most unusual skill of dead-heading roses with his tail.

When Little Chap arrived for one of his regular visits, William was so pleased to see him that he almost loved him to death - not realising that Little Chap is an unreformed alcoholic and thinks that this is the Betty Ford Clinic. He needs to rest and be left well alone.

'Bugger this for a lark,' he said and disappeared into the night once more. I hope he comes back - he needs us.

And then William disappeared, for two whole days. We were distraught. The house just wasn't the same. It was neat and tidy and boring as hell. Thermal and Tigger looked everywhere.

Then yesterday, as I was gardening, William burst in through the gate with such a tale to tell. He told it to me and he told it to Aileen, then he went and told it to the other two cats.

Then he broke a vase. But what the hell. I never liked it anyway.

22.

A MOUNTAIN OUT OF A VOLE HILL.

I didn't know what to do. I was sitting at my desk, thinking beautiful thoughts, when this rather small and, it must be said, incredibly stupid vole, marched in to my study, sat down on the hearthrug and began to polish his whiskers.

This vole was not a vole destined to explore the dizzy heights of higher education. He certainly hadn't taken an

'O' level in survival techniques.

There were three cats in the room at the time. Thermal was fast asleep on my desk, serving as combination paper weight and book rest.

Tigger was fast asleep on the fax machine, her tail tucked inside the paper guide, so that if I had needed to send a fax she would probably have gone along with it.

William, for reasons known only to himself, was sitting in the fireplace, staring up the chimney. He does that a lot recently. It's his new hobby. We have chimneys in practically every room and William has stared up them all - for hours on end. One day he will appear on University Challenge.

'William Cat - reading chimneys.'

I sat as still as I could, which is very still. I am extremely good at sitting still. I have been practising ever since I was a child. So had the vole apparently. Or maybe he was on some illegal substance. Whatever it was it certainly wasn't speed.

He sat on the hearthrug, inches away from William's tail and inspected the quality of the weave. Not of William's tail - of the rug. It's Chinese and I am very fond of it. It's the only hearthrug that never leaves its post. All the others creep surreptitiously around the house during the day and have to be rounded up and sorted out next morning.

I thought about what to do. If I made a move I would wake Thermal and Tigger, William would turn around and the vole would be history. What would David Attenborough do in a situation like this?

Well if his past record is anything to go by he would nip behind the nearest bush and whisper sweet nothings into a microphone whilst the three cats tore the poor little devil to pieces and I wasn't having that.

Tigger's glass water bowl was on the floor by my foot. The other two share a bowl in the kitchen, but Tigger doesn't share with anyone. She says it isn't hygienic. She read it in a book somewhere.

Very slowly I bent down and picked it up. I had filled it less than an hour ago and now I needed it empty. As quietly as I could I trickled the water in to the waste-paper bin, it seemed to take forever and sounded so loud that I was sure it would wake them up.

Thermal opened just the one eye and glared at me in disgust.

'For goodness sake use the litter tray.'

But Tigger woke up with a start and as she did when a fax came through. This is always the highlight of her day, it's what she lives for. She jumped down and began to attack the paper for having the sheer temerity to squeeze its way out of our machine.

William strolled over to let her know that he was there if she needed him and at that point the vole suddenly realised what a mess he'd got himself into.

He almost had kittens. Fortunately he ran over towards me to have them and as he hesitated for a moment, wondering how best to negotiate the north face of my desk, I dropped the glass bowl over the top of him.

The fax was forgotten. Tigger and William raced over to see what the hell was going on and Thermal leapt off the desk to join them.

I must say I was rather impressed with myself and I was even more impressed with the vole when I joined the cats and studied him at close hand.

Distorted by the glass his head seemed to fill the entire bowl, it looked enormous. He snarled and the cats backed away, it was the first time they had seen a sabre-toothed vole.

'What the hell is it?'

'I've no idea, but don't get too close.'

I slipped a clipboard under the bowl and carried it down to the courtyard, where I let him go. He was off like a shot and I trailed back up to the office.

Thermal was asleep on my desk, Tigger flat out on the fax machine and William was staring up the chimney.

I think I might get a pet vole. They're more fun.

23.

SPECIAL DELIVERY.

That first cup of tea in the morning has become something of an event in our house. Switch off the alarm and let the cats out. Then switch on the kettle and the television and settle down. Not for the early morning news. We have our own exclusive television programme first thing.

Ever since we installed a couple of close-circuit television cameras, one in the courtyard, the other beaming down the front path, we have had our own early morning floorshow.

The milk boy is a non event, merely a warm up for the real thing. The paper boy is a marked improvement, at least he brings a scruffy little dog along with him and it always stops for a pee up against the gatepost on the way out.

But the star turn is undoubtedly the postman, and the cats enjoy him every bit as much as we do. Tigger and William wait for him on the back step while Thermal positions himself high up on the gatepost, serving as a lookout.

If he gets into position early enough he can also glare down at the paperboy's dog as it lifts its leg and the steam begins to rise.

'I don't know. Where are the standards nowadays?'

The postman is one of those rare contented souls who knows he has the best job in the world and wouldn't swop it for anything. He loves the sun when it shines, the rain is good for his complexion and a six-inch fall of snow only serves to remind him of his childhood.

'Takes you back, doesn't it?'

Best of all he loves Thermal. As soon as the postman turns into the lane, Thermal jumps down to meet him and the two of them embark on a serious head-stroking and ankle-rubbing session before striding up the path together, side by side.

As they turn in to the courtyard, camera one hands over to camera number two and every morning Aileen and I watch as Thermal runs ahead to have a word with the odd couple waiting on the back step.

'He's coming.'

I don't think William has the slightest idea what he's talking about. William's short term memory can just about cope with the fact that he lives here and surely it must be dinner-time any minute now. His long term memory, if he has any such thing, certainly doesn't reach as far back as yesterday.

But even so he gets very excited the moment he sees the postman turn the corner, mainly because Tigger gets very excited and William thinks that it must be the thing to do.

'Hello there young lady.'

Tigger preens herself at this and allows the postman to stroke her head.

'And how are you, young man?'

William immediately falls flat on his back with all four

legs stuck high in the air, waiting to have his tummy rubbed. It's all or nothing with William and Thermal can't be doing with it.

'Pull yourself together man.'

He's anxious for the real business of the day to begin and that is when the postman first pulls the letters from his bag.

'Now let's see. What have we got for you today?'

He lets them sniff at each and every letter in turn as he sorts them out, Thermal has first sniff and Tigger the second. William has no idea what is required of him so he sniffs Tigger's bottom instead and gets a belt round the earhole for his trouble.

'This one's addressed to you Thermal.'

'Probably a fan letter.'

'And there's one for your boss.'

'Probably a bill.'

Thermal takes his sniffing very seriously. He starts with the nearest corner, then works his way along the edge, finishing up with a prolonged nasal examination of the stamp. Tigger contents herself with just a single corner and a quick rub of her cheek. William looks bemused.

The process can go on for some time, but the postman wouldn't dream of taking a shortcut. Every letter gets a personal sniff and then the cats watch with bated breath as he pops it in through the letter box.

Thermal sees the postman off the premises while Tigger bursts in to tell us that the mail has arrived. William sits on the step and plays with his rubber band.

The Post Office must lose a million rubber bands a day.

William now has seven of them. He's never had anything of his own before and he's very proud of his collection.

And I'm very proud of William – he's a trier.

24.

PANDERING TO THE GOURMETS.

I am beginning to think I spoil my cats. When they first move in, they will mop up anything I put in front of them and I am able to clear out all those tins that have worked their way to the back of the cupboard over the past few months, the ones that had the long-term residents turning up their collective nose.

'I don't think so, do you?'

'Wouldn't touch it with a barge pole, myself.'

Even Little Chap is becoming more sophisticated. When he first arrived, he would plunge his head deep into a saucer of mixed leftovers and the other three cats would sit and watch, dumbstruck and awestruck, as he seemed to take in as much through his nose and his ears as he did through his mouth.

But then I was stupid enough to give him a tin of Sainsbury's tuna, and ever since then, he has stalked upstairs first thing in the morning to discuss the day's menu with me in my office.

'Ah. Just the man I was looking for.'

In a few short months he has become the Ainsley Harriott of the cat world, and it's driving me mad.

'I thought perhaps a chicken leg with a side salad. Do we have any Feta cheese by any chance?'

The trouble is that I am already the proud owner of a Persil-white Keith Floyd and a tortoiseshell Delia Smith, and I can't be dealing with any more.

Thankfully, William is still going through his Ryan Giggs period at the moment and is no trouble whatsoever. He dribbles a lot, but that's about it...

Tigger has always had exotic tastes. She keeps an open packet of Walkers barbecued beef and onion crisps on the low shelf by the wine rack, jammed in between a set of Japanese tea cups that look very pretty but are far too small to be of any use.

I watched her in action the other morning. Thermal tagged along behind. He has never been able to manage a whole barbecued beef and onion crisp on his own - they make his eyes water - but he quite likes to mop up the crumbs afterwards.

Tigger reached a paw through the gallery rail and expertly plucked from the packet a large fat crisp, a healthy young male by the look of him, and then she hurled it over her shoulder on to the carpet by the dining table.

She's learned over the years that a cat hasn't been engineered for eating crisps on a smooth kitchen floor. They tend to lie flat, hugging the lino, and her nose gets in the way as she chases them round as she would an ice hockey puck, whereas on the carpet they lodge in the pile, standing till and proud, just asking for it.

She steadied the crisp between her two front paws and then nibbled delicately all round the outside edge until she had reduced it from a reasonable facsimile of Greenland down to an absolutely perfect scale model of the Isle of Man.

Then she turned it upside down and finished it off, starting at the Point of Ayre and working her way up towards Castletown, leaving Thermal to mop up the port of Douglas as far inland as Union Mills and as far north as Onchan while she ambled over to the shelf for seconds.

Every now and then I put my foot down. I open a couple of anonymous tins and plant the contents on the kitchen floor.

"There you are. It's either that or nothing." The trouble is it's usually nothing. They sit in a line, a good foot away from the dish, not even deigning to look in the right direction.

I can pick them up and move them a foot nearer the saucer, and yet when I let go, they are still sitting where they were originally, a good 12 inches away. I don't know how they do it. I have tried leaving it there all day until they would have needed a hammer and chisel to fight their way through the thick black crust. But it's no good. I have never been a leader of men and as far as my cats are concerned. I am merely a private in their personal Catering Corps. So before long out comes yet another tin of tuna, a couple of chicken legs and a packet of fresh mince. Surely I can do something interesting with this lot. Now where did I put that sprig of fresh parsley?

25.

FLEAS FLEA IN A SNOW STORM.

Little Chap comes and goes. He'd been gone for quite a while and we were happy to have him back again. He sat under the dining room table and scratched those parts that even a Russian gymnast would have had trouble reaching. We have a problem with Little Chap. Whenever he returns from one of his journeys into the unknown, he brings with him a whole lorry load of fleas and seems quite happy to have them on board.

"A flea isn't just for Christmas, you know - it's for life." The others sit in amazement and watch him as he bites, scratches and gouges. This is his hobby, this is what lie is good at, and over the years, he has turned himself into a master craftsman.

159

Nevertheless I can't be doing with it under my dining table and I was just about to sort him out when Aileen appeared wearing her satin robe and a half-baked expression.

"Little Chap's back." I told her.

"I know. I could hear him scratching. He woke me up."

I made her a cup of tea and poured a drop in a saucer for Thermal. He took a delicate sip and then frowned.

"You've forgotten the sweetener."

Aileen took a sip from her cup and grimaced.

"I know. I've forgotten the sweetener." But I hadn't forgotten about Little Chap. I like to get hold of him as soon as he thumps in through the cat flap.

At least he's the only one who will have anything to do with the flea powder. The others run a mile.

Thermal takes off first thing every morning, the minute I

pick up a can of deodorant.

They have been spoilt rotten. They prefer to go private, demanding either a little drop of Tiguvon on the back of the neck or a small dash of Program as part of a calorie-controlled diet.

Little Chap isn't as fussy, mainly because he has no idea what on earth is going on.

If I brush him for a moment or two, he disappears into a world of his own - his mouth falls wide open and his body relaxes to such a state that at any moment, I almost expect one of his legs to drop off.

At this point I reach out for the can of flea powder and the other cats take cover behind the sideboard, doing their best to warn him of the coming danger.

'Look out. He's behind you.'

But a little scrub at the base of his tail will make sure

that Little Chap stays safely tucked away in Never-

Never Land and before long I can hear the fleas

coughing and choking.

'My chest feels just like sandpaper.'

'There's a lot of it going about.'

But this time the hole in the canister was all bunged up

and so I had to improvise.

I massaged Little Chap with my knee while I poked the

hole free with the thin wire stalk of a Christmas tree

bauble.

It took a bit of doing, but in the end it worked a treat and

then I gave him the full monty.

I kept my finger on the button for ages. If a job's worth

doing, it's worth doing well - but the effect, as they say

in the ads, was shattering.

He had a narrow white line right down the length of his

back and his tail. One moment I was dealing with an affectionate, albeit flea-ridden moggie, and the next I was the proud owner of a small, but beautifully marked skunk.

He couldn't believe it. He stood up, took one look at himself and sat down again.

'What on earth have you done?' Well, how can you explain to a cat that you have just sprayed him with artificial snow?

I couldn't believe I could have been so stupid. I made a grab for him so that I could put matters right, but he was off and out through the cat flap before you could say Jack Frost.

It didn't take long to find him. We don't have all that many skunks in Huddersfield and my neighbour was surprised to see one sitting on her kitchen windowsill.

The good thing about Little Chap is that he doesn't bear a grudge and I'm sure he will forgive me eventually. I'm not so sure about the small herd of albino fleas who were unfortunately caught in the cross-fire.

My neighbour poured me a cup of coffee as I combed out a small black-cat on her hearth rug.

"Have you finished your Christmas decorations yet?"

"No." I told her. "I've only just started."

26.

STRIKING THE LOTTERY.

I can always tell when Mrs Hattersley is standing on the

front step. She has a way of making the doorbell sound

depressed. The postman has it chirruping away

optimistically - it sounds glad to be alive at the touch of

his finger. But the moment the doorbell sees Mrs

Hattersley coming up the path, it begins to feel its age

and withdraws within itself. Aileen didn't even look up from her bacon sandwich.

"That must be Mrs Hattersley."

She wouldn't come in. She never does. But would I pop over there - she had something she wanted me to look at.

I'm always popping over there. Throughout the winter I bleed her radiators for her on a weekly basis and pluck the fluff from her vacuum cleaner all the year round. She still has to grasp the notion that the bag has to be emptied every now and then and so my job is to poke out the tubes with the wrong end of the yard brush.

"I'll be over in a minute. Soon as I've fed the cats."

And that's easier said than done. They've become very fussy of late.

Thermal just picks at his food nowadays, unless it is

very expensive and initially intended for human consumption. And I was also convinced that Tigger was fast becoming anorexic until I noticed that she seemed to be putting on weight by the hour.

Even William has cut down on his consumption of Whiskas chunks in gravy by at least a hundred-weight a day. He didn't even bother to turn up for breakfast this morning. It's very worrying.

He nipped out for a quick pee in the shrubbery and never came back.

So I left him an overflowing saucer by the cat flap and popped over to see what Mrs Hattersley had in store for me. It was her toaster. It couldn't cope with her white sliced bread and that's not the sort of behaviour you expect from a toaster. There's very little else they are capable of doing and you can't have them just loafing about.

"It barely warms the bread."

I soon had it sorted out and back on the job. I turned the little knob up from nought to three and a half and we had a trial run.

"That's wonderful."

She thinks I'm a mechanical genius and I don't like to disillusion her. I also try not to stay for a cup of tea, but this time there was no escape.

She had buttered me the slice of toast as a special reward and so we went through to the lounge and huddled round the fire.

"Mind the cat."

I didn't know she had a cat, but she did. It was William, all curled up on the hearthrug and fast asleep with an empty dish beside him. A Pyrex dish, the sort you might use if you were making a rice pudding for six people, and William had licked it clean.

"He's a stray, poor thing," said Mrs Hattersley. "I don't think he'd ever had a square meal before he started coming round here."

The poor starving stray gave his limbs a luxurious stretch and then marched over to the bowl to see if by any chance he'd missed the odd morsel.

Mrs Hattersley sprang to her feet. "He's still hungry you see. I'm trying to build him up."

He was about to explode at any moment now and she was trying to build him up. Apparently her late husband was a butcher and the new people who had taken over the shop saw that she wanted for nothing.

"He's very fond of mince and he likes a pork chop every now and then. The others just stick to the mince."

"The others?'

At the sound of my voice William swung round and I have never seen a cat look more embarrassed.

He walked straight past the dish as though he had never seen it before in his life and then strode out of the room, passing Thermal on his way in.

"Here's his friend," said Mrs Hattersley "I'll just get him a bite to eat."

We've sorted it all out. She'd also been feeding a tortoiseshell cat, quite a lady by all accounts, and she had no idea the three of them were mine and I suppose it's understandable. After all, she's only been living four doors away for the past 11 years.

I've found her a genuine stray. I'm picking him up on Wednesday. He thinks he's won the lottery.

170

27.

What's there to laugh about?

Spring is just around the corner and I hope it doesn't hang about. It can't come soon enough for me.

The cats have gone stir crazy. Thermal has taken to sitting in my wastepaper basket for hours on end. He just sits there in the corner of my office, his little chin hanging limply over the basketwork edge, his eyes glazed by a mixture of boredom and cheap whisky.

I can't concentrate. I have a screenplay to finish. But as soon as I switch on the computer, a deep sigh spills from over in the corner and those big blue eyes almost drown me in a pool of misery.

'There must be more to life than this.'

'Oh for goodness sake, cheer up.'

He's given up on his hobbies. He doesn't even bother to play with his catnip mouse any more and his live-in sultana is considering filing for a divorce on the grounds of desertion.

If it were just Thermal alone I would have had him up to the vets by now for a shot of something, but the others are just the same.

Tigger sits on the windowsill, staring out at the passing

grey days, glumly watching the sleet and the rain as it bounces off the glass.

She's never been like this before. Last year she was out in the courtyard all day long, thumping the living daylights out of any passing snow flake who had the temerity to think it could possibly land in our yard.

Thermal dealt with the Autumn leaves, shepherding them in to a corner by the dustbin, and between them they did a pretty good job of repelling all boarders - but not this year.

Even William has caught the bug. His energy level is still pumped up to gas mark 37, but he expends it all by racing from window to window to see how it's going on out there. There are seventeen of them to be checked and when he's done them all he collapses in a miserable heap and sighs a sigh that comes right up from his black and white boots.

'Fwooooow!'

'Come on now - you're a pain in the neck, the lot of you.'

Every now and then the odd squirrel pops over from the park to try and cheer them up - and we do have some very odd squirrels over there.

There's one we know only as Gerald. We haven't been formally introduced, he's too quick on his feet for that, but he certainly looks like a Gerald to me and he comes over occasionally to entertain the troops.

This week he rather fancied a peanut. Not just any old peanut, he wanted the one that was half sticking out through the bars of the bird's dispenser. It does look awfully tempting, but you can't shift it - it's been there for ages. The birds have tried and I have tried, but there's no way. It's there for the duration.

But Gerald wouldn't have it. He pushed and he pulled, a half nelson here and a full throttle there. He even tried a Chinese burn but the peanut wasn't having any of it. He should have brought a spanner with him.

And all this time the sparrows and tits were playing hell with him.

'Get *off - it's ours. We can show you the receipt.'*

Gerald's language is rather blue at the best of times and for him this was the worst of times. The air turned a sort of sapphire as he fought them off, but then they went and had a word with a magpie friend of theirs and even Gerald had to admit defeat.

The magpie came at him like Thunderbird two and

Gerald sensibly dropped like a stone, ten feet down on to the courtyard.

'Come and look at this,' I shouted to the cats. But the gloom seems to have penetrated their very bones. They didn't want to know.

Thermal's chin sank deeper in to the basket and Tigger sank into that strange position where all her legs disappear underneath her and it looks as though she's about to hatch a nest full of eggs. Her forehead clonked miserably down on the table top and from the hearthrug William gave a deep sigh.

'Fwooooow.'

I grabbed my jacket from off the back of my chair.

'Wait for me Gerald. I'm coming with you.'

I'll be back in the Spring.

28.

SO, WHO NEEDS TO NAP ANYWAY?

It always cheers me up. The sight of four little bottoms settling themselves down for a communal lunch. Tigger invariably leads the way and then takes the saucer on the left, first a perfunctory sniff and then a delicate nibble.

'What is it, Tigger?'

This is the moment of truth. Tigger has the palate of a wine taster and the others trust her judgement implicitly. She rolls the tuna and chicken around her tongue and

Thermal waits expectantly for her decision. I pray that she won't spit it out.

'Tuna I think - with possibly a hint of chicken on the side.'

There's a collective sigh. Thermal could sigh for England.

'Oh not again. Has the man no imagination?'

Tigger wiggles her bottom and settles down to the job in hand. Nibbling delicately around the edges in a very feminine manner. She reminds me of the Queen Mother. Her greatest regret is that she hasn't been engineered to hold a knife and fork properly,

'It's quite pleasant - if a little unadventurous.'

Now that they have the go-ahead the others tuck in, and there's no nibbling delicately around the edges. When you watch him in action there's no doubting that Thermal is a man, but you could take him anywhere and he wouldn't let you down. He's the sort of man women say it's a pleasure to cook for. He's started - so he's going to finish. But at least he takes a breath every now and again. Not like William. He really ought to wear a diver's helmet and a rubber suit with lead lined boots. He plunges his head deep in to the tuna and chicken, coming up for air only once during the average saucerful, twice if he's lucky enough to have been given the red Pyrex bowl.

Little Chap has a style all of his own. For a start he eats standing up. Maybe it's because he has spent so much of his life eating food that wasn't his in the first place, in places he shouldn't have been in - in the second place. When he first arrived he used to eat looking over his shoulder all the time. Ever on the look-out for the returning owner, or the owner of the owner, which could turn out to be an even more painful experience.

He is a much more relaxed cat these days, but he still stands to attention when he eats - ready to make his escape at the slightest sound.

William is always the first to empty his saucer and always the last to leave. He incurs more penalty points than the others and so has to spend precious time on a mopping up operation, clearing the flying debris from around his saucer.

The others usually wait for him to finish, pointing out bits he's missed here and there and then it's time for that great British institution - the afternoon nap. This is not to be confused with the early morning nap, the mid-morning nap or the late morning nap. It's an entirely different sort of nap and has much more in common with mid-afternoon nap and the early evening snooze.

Now that spring has sprung they often take their afternoon nap outside in the courtyard and if I'm very good I am allowed to join in.

Not on the lovers' bench that Aileen bought me as a present for my birthday last year - Tigger sleeps there and she needs the room. And not on the stone mushroom either. Apparently Thermal has paid a years rent in advance for the privilege and has the receipt to prove it somewhere, if only he could lay his paws on it.

William's naps are fleeting affairs and use up a great deal of energy. He chases the pale sunshine from paving stone to paving stone as it works its way across the courtyard. Flinging himself down on his back, all four legs in the air, his white undercarriage soaking up just a couple of minutes of solar power before the fickle rays decide to move on.

He can get through as many as thirty paving stones in an hour and it's an exhausting business. He has to go inside afterwards and have a lie down.

Little Chap always takes to the window sill high up on the balcony. From there he can keep a watchful eye on things, while the other eye tucks itself up and has a few moments off.

I usually finish up sitting on the back door step. But never mind. Who wants a nap when there's so much going on?

29.

ALL SHAPES AND SIZES.

Mrs Bairstow rested her ample bosom on the gatepost and stared at the cats, who were scattered all over the courtyard.

Thermal and William were doing a little light gardening at either end of the rockery - one digging a custom built privy by the sweetly smelling chives, while the other had already finished and was making himself busy, filling in and patting down.

Little Chap sat on the window sill, staring in. He does that. After a night spent fast asleep on the dining room table, he then goes out first thing in the morning and stares in - at the dining room table. He's not one for scenery, isn't Little Chap.

Tigger sat on the vacant gatepost staring across at Mrs Bairstow's bosom, wondering why she bothered to lug it about with her everywhere she went. Mrs Bairstow's bosom is bigger than all four cats put together and so Tigger didn't get too close. You can never tell - she didn't have it on a lead and it might turn nasty if approached.

I listened to all the local gossip and then, as the well began to run dry, Mrs Bairstow seemed to notice the cats for the first time.

'Funny little things, aren't they? They come in all shapes and sizes.'

Well no, they don't actually. They are all shaped like cats. I have never had one yet that wasn't shaped like a cat. Someone once said that Arthur bore a startling resemblance to a young camel, but that was only in a certain light and on days when his arthritis was playing him up. But they do come in assorted sizes - and that includes the size of their brains.

Tigger is university material. She speaks several languages including Siamese, both blue point and chocolate tortie. She's fluent in Turkish Van and Persian and has a smattering of Abyssinian, which unfortunately she doesn't get to use all that often in Huddersfield.

She can also get by in both Chinchilla and Angora and since William came to live with us her broad Yorkshire has come on in leaps and bounds. Her standard English isn't as good as it might be. She has never been able to understand the meaning of the word no for instance - but then my British Shorthair isn't what it ought to be, so who am I to talk?

She also has an honours degree in radiators and can tell to the minute which one will come on when and for how long. The others have never quite mastered the art and so whenever Tigger makes a move, they all get up and follow - in a line, like a string of hairy ducklings.

'She's very clever, isn't she?'

'Got it down to a fine art.'

Thermal on the other hand has learned everything he

knows from the university of life. Or the University of the Nine Lives, as he likes to put it. He says he's used up twelve of them already, but then maths was never one of his strong points.

He's a past master at being stuck up trees, getting himself trapped beneath floorboards and locked in garages. He once studied guttering very closely for a day and a half until someone found a ladder long enough to reach him, three storeys up.

And yet he's probably the brightest of them all. Not as academically inclined as Tigger, I have yet to see him reading a book - but he's as sharp as a new pin and he's certainly got the gift of the gab.

Little Chap on the other hand has come up through the school of hard knocks. He graduated with PhD in cat-flap technology, an eye for the ladies and a left ear shaped like a dried apricot.

Unfortunately his reputation as a ladies man suffered a steep decline after a visit to the vet, but it would probably have taken a dive anyway as his right ear is now shaped like a dried prune and he's more suited to character parts than that of leading man.

Nevertheless he's as bright as a button and generous to a fault. He'd share his last flea with anyone and often does.

And then of course there's William. He fluffed his exams in Kittengarten. He got a D in grooming and an F minus in eating nicely, but he managed a B plus for purring enthusiastically and that's what life is all about. All in all, they're shaping up rather well.

30.

Buffy the Cat Slayer - Not.

She took up most of the doorway. Her huge shadow painting the mosaic tiled floor solid black, until eventually it ran out of puff and gave up, over by the combined boot scraper and umbrella stand.

'I'm fed up to the teeth with them,' she blustered. 'They're forever in my garden. They camp there all afternoon like a bunch of boy scouts.'

I promised to do what I could - though I didn't know what I could do. Confiscate Thermal's Swiss-army knife perhaps, or threaten to re-adjust Little Chap's toggle if ever he set foot on Mrs Cartwright's lawn again.

'I can't keep them on a lead you know.'

'Well if I catch them at it once more, I'll set the dog on them.'

She stormed off down the path and I managed to keep a straight face until I had closed the door tight behind her and shut myself in the kitchen.

Set the dog on them. Have you seen her dog? No of course you haven't - that's a silly question. It's one of those miniature white poodles. He's had his middle shaved like a belly dancer, he wears a couple of pairs of sculptured plus fours and has a stringy little tail with a great big furry bobble on the end.

I know it's not the dog's fault and I know that despite being made to look a right Charlie by their owners, some of these poodles are very tough little devils indeed. I suppose they have to be, looking like that - but not this one.

His name is Buffy and he's still suffering nightmares from having once barked at Tigger in what he supposed to be an aggressive fashion.

'I beg your pardon. Are you addressing me by any chance?'

'Woof.'

He never knew what hit him. One minute he was poncing down the path like a Vivienne Westwood model swaying down the catwalk, the next he was upside down in the catmint with a very sore nose and an ego to match.

It's the catmint of course that draws the cats over there, time after time. There are acres of the stuff, completely surrounding a huge sunken lawn that hosts a rough rustic bird table, an old stone birdbath and is at all times covered with the crumbs of at least four loaves of bread with the crusts cut off, for those older birds who have lost their teeth and are afraid of heights.

And it's the ideal spot for my four furry ornithologists to spend a sunny summer's afternoon. They lie on their backs, soaking up the sun and breathing in the catmint.

'Hey man - this is the real stuff.'

Buffy glares fiercely from the other side of the french windows, his mouth opening and shutting silently as he yelps at them from behind the safety of the double glazing.

'Yeah. Roll me another joint. That dog's over there's beginning to look damned attractive. Just love those cute little pyjamas.'

They rarely catch a bird. About once a year they come across an ancient sparrow, an old-aged pensioner complete with zimmer frame, who just happens to be studying a pamphlet on euthanasia at the time, but generally they are far too stoned on the catmint to give a damn about anything as active as hunting, shooting or fishing.

I wish I had trained them properly, but it's too late now. I have just met a cat called Henry - he's an actor and he's playing the part of my mother's cat in my screenplay *of*

Lost For Words (On ITV in the Autumn - seats in all parts.)

Henry has to sit still for ages, surrounded by a dozen actors all chatting at once. He has to jump off a sink, run behind a settee and tuck himself under Dame Thora Hird's arm until she drops him with a dull thud on to the doorstep. It took seven takes and he never complained once.

He's a star and I told Thermal about him.

'What's the money like?'

'Pretty good.'

'I could have done that.'

'No you couldn't. You would have run off and hidden in the scenery. Anyway - you're the wrong colour.'

'That's racial discrimination, that is.'

'Don't be ridiculous.'

'I could have you for that.'

But I don't think I need to worry. One word from me and the police will have him for being in possession of catmint with a street value of over twenty-three pence. They'd lock him up and throw away the key.

It's a tough business show business. Even if you do sleep with the author.

31.

TECHNICOLOUR CATS

This is weird. I'm sitting at my desk, a coffee in one hand, a cigarette in the other, and I am surrounded by an entire herd of multi-coloured cats.

There's a red one over by the fireplace and a bright blue one lying flat on his back on the table in the window. Another red one, of a slightly more crimson hue this time, is fast asleep on that bit that sticks out from the bookcase and there's a green and yellow striped tortoiseshell just below him, stretched out on the carpet.

For a moment I wonder what sort of cigarette I am smoking. Have Dunhill started putting something in them?

'Aileen come and look at this.'

Which is a pretty stupid thing to say to a woman who is registered blind and can't see her hand before her face.

'What?'

'The cats. They're all sorts of colours. Thermal's gone blue.'

A look of horror passed across her face. For a moment she wondered if he might have stopped breathing. Should she give him the kiss of life?

'It's the stained glass windows, love. The cats have each picked out a different spot of sunlight and now they're all the colours of the rainbow.'

As the sun shifted its position in the sky, the cats shifted their position in the room, seeking out fresh pastures in which to soak up the warmth. Tigger moved a foot to her left and instantly turned a bright emerald green. Thermal, half in the sunshine and half out, swopped his electric blue duffle coat for a pair of tailored jogging pants in a rather fetching shade of pale lilac.

It was as though I had been transported to some sort of Alice in Wonderland world where anything was possible, especially when William glared at me through a pair of deep green eyes that clashed awfully with the orange tips of his whiskers.

He had looked so much better before technicolour arrived, back in the old black and white days when cats were cats and not some sort of mobile fashion accessory.

Then Thermal shifted position once more, this time slipping into a little pale pink number with adjustable shoulder straps and matching bootees. It took me back to the time some years ago, when a bottle of home-made damson wine exploded just as he happened to be trotting past the wine rack in the kitchen.

The cork shot out and the damson wine followed. Thermal was only a slip of a thing at the time and he instantly turned in to a bright purple slip of a thing. He was soaked from head to toe and he shot out of the house.

By the time he came back home he had licked most of it off. He was now a delicate pink with broad irregular stripes and he was stoned out of his mind.

We had no idea how to sober him up. You can't give a

six-month old kitten a mug of strong black coffee and then walk him round the block. So I sponged him down and he slept it off.

Maybe I should have written to the experts at *Your Cat Questions*. It would have made a pleasant change from spraying and fleas.

Q My six month-old kitten comes home drunk as a skunk, every Friday night. What should I do?

A Try smearing butter on his paws. If that doesn't work, give him a sharp clip round the earhole.

Of course if I had really wanted to freak them out I could have told them that my white shorthaired cat had recently changed into a bright fluorescent green shorthaired cat with orange front paws and that he was sitting up and glaring at me.

Which he is, right now. Thermal has an inbuilt digital alarm clock situated somewhere towards his rear. It must have been fashioned on the lines of those silent mobile phones that vibrate when a call is coming through.

At twelve o'clock on the dot he stands up, shakes his back leg a couple of times and glares at me.

'Lunch.'

The others rely on him. As soon as they see that back leg trembling they haul themselves to their collective feet and glare at me in unison.

'Lunch.'

Or at least, that's what it sounds like. I have never dared take a chance on it. So I had better go and feed them now. I've got them a nice bit of stewing steak. That should bring the colour back to their cheeks.

32.

DERIC'S WAKE-UP CALL.

I don't know whether I'm coming or going at the moment. I hardly had any sleep again last night. I could kill those damn birds.

There are two of them. A tall one and a short one and they sit on the chimney stack, by the skylight, and wake me with a start at twenty-two minutes past four every blessed morning.

The tall one is into light opera and performs selected excerpts from The Desert Song and Madam Butterfly, while the short one is a throwback from the old music hall days. He's brought his act up to date and now specializes in impressions of mobile phones, selected excerpts from Nokia and Ericsson, and one day I'm going to wring his blessed neck.

They also have a friend who visits every now and then. His conversation is somewhat limited. He bellows *'Hello Kevin'* at six minute intervals, but it must have been his morning off.

I used to be able to cope with this early morning bombardment. Get up, make a quick cup of tea, light a cigarette and read the boring bits I skipped from yesterday's *Daily Telegraph.* Then back to bed within twenty minutes and sleep like a log until just before eight.

But not anymore. Not since we had the new burglar alarm installed. Now all the interior doors have to be shut up tight last thing at night and I can't roam around the house like I used to. So I'm stuck up there with the three tenors.

The cats can't cope with it either. Tigger has always made a habit of sleeping on the top shelf in the airing cupboard and then, as daylight comes creeping in through the window, she jumps down, polishes off any leftover titbits, and trots upstairs to join us in bed at around five in the morning.

Thermal has always curled up on the fax machine just before midnight and then, after sharpening his claws by shredding any overnight communications into a thousand pieces, he trots upstairs and joins us in bed at around five in the morning.

William's routine has always been slightly more complicated. He has made a habit of dropping off to sleep with his chin resting on the edge of his dish by the kitchen door - he's quite partial to a midnight snack, it keeps his blood sugar up apparently, and so he finds it very handy to go to sleep with his head in the saucer. It saves time when he wakes up.

Once he's licked his dish down to the pattern he goes and sits in the sink for few moments and has a refreshing drink from under the dripping tap. This can take ages and seems a pretty stupid thing to do since there is a bowl of water available twenty-four hours a day, just by the big brass thing with three legs that Aileen bought in a car boot sale - the one that we are going to find out what it's for one of these days.

Aileen is always telling me that I should fit a new washer to the tap, but then I would have to take William to one side and explain what I've gone and done in words of one syllable and I'm not really up to the hassle of all that at the moment. He's very good with his paws, but complex technical details just bounce off him.

Anyway - once he's had his late night snack and his drink of water, he has his mad half hour. I don't know what he gets up to, but I have heard him at it.

It sounds as though he first strips off all the wallpaper, knocks down an interior wall and then, after carting a load of breeze blocks all the way across the kitchen floor, he builds a small annexe with a south facing aspect.

Funnily enough though he never leaves any mess, so he

must clear up after himself before he trots upstairs and joins us in bed at around five in the morning.

But all good things must come to an end and now the lot of us are confined to our quarters for the duration. Thermal had an idea.

'Just put a cat flap in every door.'

'What about me, then?'

'Very big cat flaps, with lots of room.'

But I think we'll have to give in graciously and just get used to it. It's all very sad - five o'clock in the morning will never be the same again.

33.

RETAIL THERAPY.

Tigger and I were watching QVC, the shopping channel. They had a special offer on beauty treatments and we both like to keep ourselves nice.

Aileen had left the set switched on while she popped round next door and so Tigger I popped in to her office for a quick cigarette and a vitamin tablet. I smoked the cigarette and Tigger had the vitamin tablet. She must be on about twenty a day at the moment and I keep telling her it's time she cut down.

QVC has changed Aileen's life. With her limited sight she can't make out the jewellery that adorns her own fingers, or even see that which hangs from around her neck. Earrings are one of life's great mysteries for her and so she has always relied upon my expert description as we gaze in through the jeweller's window.

'It's a sort of bluey-green stone, with a sort of gold thingy all around it.'

But on the shopping channel they have huge close ups and, if she puts her nose right up to the screen, the pendants and rings are twenty-seven inches across. It's wonderful. She can almost see the lobster-claw fastening on today's special offer and a sharp click on the mute button does away with all that waffling and blathering that unfortunately comes along with the pictures. A short telephone call and she has added yet another item to her collection.

Tigger and I aren't all that interested in jewellery. Tigger once owned a flea collar that glowed in the dark and it put her off for life. It put me off for life as well. Once you've been woken in the early hours of the morning by a flea collar, hovering all on its own about six inches above your chest, it does tend to put you off.

And rings and ankle bracelets aren't much use if you are a cat. They drop off. They aren't designed to stay on any limb which will eventually finish up as a paw, and pearl earrings would look a bit daft on a pair of pointed ears that stick straight up in the air.

Tigger did once think about having her navel pierced,

but I pointed out the fact that no one would be able to see it.

'They would when I roll on my back.'

'You'd have to have your tummy shaved.'

She'd had that done once before, when we'd taken her to the vet to be seen to, and she shuddered at the thought and so we were both pleased when the beauty products came on, especially when the first item was a shampoo that added a silvery touch of brightness to grey hair.

'That would be good for you.'

She's very thoughtful.

'Your hair has gone all brassy. It could do with livening up.'

She can be too thoughtful at times.

We waited to see if they had a shampoo that added a

touch of brightness to ginger, black and white hair but apparently they haven't got round to that yet.

'There's probably no demand for it.'

'That's what they always say.'

We sat and smoked and chomped our way through an overlong demonstration of fake tanning cream.

'You could put some on your black and white bits - see if it made them ginger.'

Tigger thought that was stupid, which it was really, but she brightened up considerably when she saw the presenter demonstrating a massaging foot spa.

'What about one of those?'

It had two separate compartments, one for each foot with powerful water jets to soothe away those aches and pains.

'No good for you - you've got too many feet.'

She thought about that for a while.

'I could lie down in one side.'

'You'd get a full body massage.'

'It's a thought, isn't it?'

She also thought that we might fill the other compartment with cat litter so that it would always be on tap, so to speak.

'It would get soaked.'

She shuddered at the thought. There's nothing worse than wet cat litter.

Then just as I was beginning to think we would never find anything for her, up came the manicure set. She's always wanted one of her own. Every morning, after putting on her make-up, Aileen gently files Tigger's nose with the nail file and then buffs it up with that chamois leather thing with the handle. Tigger loves it - she's got the smartest nose in Huddersfield.

I've ordered one for her. It's her birthday next month. She's getting fed up with the Jeffrey Archer novels.

34.

PUSSY PASTIMES.

A week away from home. No cooking, no writing, no cats to feed and pamper. I missed them of course and knew they would be missing me. I rang on Wednesday, just for a quick word with Thermal, but Kealan said he had nipped out for a while and that Tigger was too busy to come to the phone at the moment.

Apparently Tigger was on guard by the laundry basket. She sits there for hours, waiting for the washing to begin. Then she insists on sniffing each and every garment before it is hurled deep in to the bowels of the washing machine. It's a sort of feline quality control and she's very good at it. She doesn't sniff them on the way out as she has become allergic to the fabric conditioner - it makes her eyes water and she says she can't taste her tuna for days afterwards.

Kealan and Claire were house-sitting for us and I knew the house would be in safe hands. They were of course also cat-sitting and here, one or two doubts were poised at the back of my mind. So I tried to make everything crystal clear.

"Thermal and William like the tuna in water, but Tigger prefers the smaller tins in brine. They are the ones on the second shelf and she has smaller portions than the other two. If you give her too much she won't touch it.

I've marked the tins of Whiskas with an indelible pencil.

With a 'Th' for Thermal and a single 'T' for Tigger.

William's are all marked with a 'W.'

Kealan turned this information over in her mind.

"Thermal is the white one, isn't he?"

I wondered for a moment if I should mark each of the

cats with an indelible pencil, but decided that would be

going a little too far.

"The Coley steaks go in the microwave for three

minutes and then let them stand for a while. The cats

prefer them hot, but not too hot. So I blow on them and

then I..."

At this point I glanced at Kealan and her eyes were

telling me that once I was out of the way, these blessed

cats would eat whatever they were damn well given and

be grateful for it. To be on the safe side, I left a long list of instructions, pointing out that Thermal liked to sleep in my office and that I always left him a midnight snack on my desk, just to the right of the letter rack. Also that I changed their water daily - from the filter tap in the kitchen, not the ordinary tap.

The more I wrote the dafter I felt, but I couldn't stop. I mentioned that Tigger slept on the fax machine and asked them not to draw the curtains, otherwise she wouldn't be able to see the cars going past; that William liked to sleep in the kitchen with his chin over… I filled two sheets of A4 paper and, as I read it over, realised what an idiot I have become over the past few years.

Kealan read the sheets slowly and passed them to Claire. "What about their ballet lessons'?"

So I left it at that and hoped that the five of them would get on well. The cats came out to see us off. They sat on the wall in a line and I could still feel their accusing eyes boring in to the back of my neck an hour later. And that's where they were when we came home. But then they marched into the house ahead of us, ignoring us completely, ducking under our vain attempts at back scratching and meeting our greetings with a stony glare. Thermal went into the lounge and sat on Kealan's knee while Tigger curled up around Claire's feet. William marched into the kitchen and fell asleep with his chin in his dish.

Aileen and I followed him and began to unpack. We'd saved them a sausage each from the Little Chef and I put them on the table. William sniffed them and sprang to life and then miraculously, two small cats strolled in from the lounge, purring and brushing against our legs. It's nice to be loved for yourself, isn't it?

35.

GREEN CLAWS.

The weather has been pretty good around here. Mild enough for Thermal and me to sit out in the front garden and pursue our separate hobbies. Mine involves the morning paper, a pack of cigarettes and a glass of red wine.

Thermals requirements are just as simple. All he needs is a small pair of steps and a leg up so that he can deadhead the roses at his leisure.

He's very good at it and getting better by the minute, but the other cats can't understand his horticultural obsession. They are into the more traditional feline pursuits such as hunting, shooting and fishing. Though I must admit I can't remember the last time they ever shot anything.

They are also heavily into the preservation of territorial rights. First thing in the morning Tigger likes to check all the hedges, sniffing at almost each and every leaf with the utmost dedication.

It's rather like a wine tasting, she sniffs delicately at first and then, gulping in the tell-tale evidence, she swishes the aroma around the back of her throat.

'Mmmm! Small short-haired kitten, female tabby with a limp in her left back leg. Passed through the hedge at

around six thirty-seven this morning, probably on her

way to do her paper round.'

Sometimes she jumps back in alarm, her eyes crossed and running with tears.

'Yuck! Denton - and he's been eating garlic again.'

William is into grates. In the house he spends most of his time peering up the chimney, listening to the birds as they warm their bums on the chimney pot, but once outside he spends hours and hours peering down the grate in the back lane.

He once spotted a small rodent and the thrill has stayed with him ever since. He sits in the gutter, still as a garden gnome, head bent in total concentration as visiting cars try to manoeuvre round him, parking almost on his tail.

Every now and then he springs into action, his paw diving

down through the bars as he sees something moving in the murky depths. I have done a few basic sums and reckon that since his front legs are roughly six inches long and the grating is some four feet deep, then whatever lives down there is more than likely to die of old age. They probably think he's waving to them.

'He seems a very friendly cat. Must go up there and have a chat with him sometime.'

Little Chap doesn't have any hobbies. Whenever he comes back to see us, after one of his many excursions, he is absolutely shattered and all he does is sleep.

I have a theory that he's got himself a job as a long distance lorry driver and it takes it out of him. I could be wrong but I do have a nose for these things.

But Thermal as I say has become a dab hand at

deadheading the roses and his commitment to the cause is a lesson to us all. It started when a wasp took a deep breath, plucked up its courage and decided to dive-bomb him, and Thermal wasn't having that. He chased it all over the garden and then moved in for the kill as it settled on the petals of a geriatric rose that had but a few hours to live.

He moved in silently and belted both rose and wasp with a crisp right hander. Whatever happened to the wasp we shall never know, but the rose gave a deep sigh and disintegrated immediately, its petals falling gracefully, showering Thermal until he looked like a bridesmaid at a posh society wedding.

That small moment changed his life forever and ever since he has kept a close eye on them. He moves through the garden tapping every rose from inexperienced bud to fully grown adult. His disappointment when they merely lean back and roll with the blow being more than compensated for when they collapse and rain petals down on his head.

Once he's sorted out the smaller bushes I go and fetch the kitchen steps for him. They're on castors and I push him around the garden as he tackles those that would otherwise be out of reach.

But now the bleak midwinter is edging in and there's only the odd rose left, hanging on by the skin of its teeth.

Still there's always Christmas to look forward to - the tree, the baubles and the fairy lights. Looks like he's going to need the steps again.

36.

TOGETHERNESS.

The birds are back, both of them. They woke me even earlier than usual this morning. I think the tall one has a cold. His voice seemed huskier than before and he had only managed to cough his way through the first few bars of Rossini's Barber of Seville before the short one cut in with his latest mobile phone impression. He has been practising call waiting for some time and he's just about got it right.

I jumped out of bed and then realised that the short one was staring in at me through the rooflight and I automatically pulled in my stomach and puffed out my chest and then felt rather daft. I thought for a moment that I might dial 1471, ring him back and tell him to push off, but in the end I decided to ignore him and go and make a cup of coffee instead.

The cats decided to ignore me as I pushed open my study door. I must have cut a ghostly figure as I crept, cup in hand, towards the table in the window. Tigger opened just the one eye and then quickly closed it again.

'Don't look chaps. He's stark naked.'

Thermal decided to chance a peep. After all these years he still hasn't worked out how I do it. He'd love to be able to strip off every now and then, on hot summer days and after he's slept too long by the radiator. He spends hours searching his undercarriage, looking for the zip, but so far he hasn't found a thing. That's not quite true - he has found a thing, but he's still looking for the zip.

He came over and joined me at the table and we stared out across the park together. There were lights cutting through the dark, dozens of them, pinpricks at first, strobing through the trees, then growing in stature as they came closer.

Thermal was transfixed. He sat in front of me, on the table with his back to me, staring out of the window, his two little ears standing to attention, framing the scene for me like a couple of bookends.

I tried to make out what was going on. What looked like

a huge spaceship emerged from the gloom then came to

rest in the centre of the park. It was as though I were

sitting in on the opening sequence of ET.

'ET go home.'

'Pardon?'

'It was a film. The hero looked a lot like you.'

Thermal preened at the thought. I hope he's not around

the next time they show it on television.

Then a splash of red and gold lettering solved the mystery.

The Moscow State Circus was with us once more and as

Thermal and I sat idly drinking our coffee, me from my

cup and Thermal from my saucer, an enormous marquee

was raised higher and higher until it was tall as my house.

By six in the morning everything was in place, as though

it had always been there. A rather sexy young acrobat in a

leopardskin bikini emerged from one of the caravans and began to practise her routine. Thermal wasn't all that impressed, but then he didn't have the binoculars.

'How about a spot of breakfast?

'Just the two of us?'

'Yes. Be like old times.'

Silently we crept from the room. Past William who was flat on his back and snoring gently. Past Tigger who had both of her front paws draped over my *Compaq* laptop, her head resting neatly on the disc drive. Past Little Chap who had velcroed himself to the radiator for the night in order to extract every last drop of warmth. Had it been switched on he would have really felt the benefit.

They don't all four usually sleep together like this. Must have had an important meeting last night. Maybe they'd had a few drinks and decided to stay the night.

Down in the kitchen Thermal leaned heavily against my ankle as I read him some interesting bits from the *Daily Telegraph.* He prefers the sport to the politics, but basically he simply likes to be involved and it took me back to the days when he was a tiny bit of a kitten and there was just the two of us.

Then the others barged in demanding their breakfast and life moved in to the fast lane once more.

Thermal and I rather enjoy our rare moments together. I think I might take him to the circus tonight.

37.

CHICKEN LICKIN'.

I popped in to the Co-op yesterday. When the store first opened they called it Leo's, but then they went upmarket and had a refit and the name changed to Pioneer. The main branch in town is now known as Living and yet everyone still calls it the Co-op. I don't know why they bother.

I pop in twice a week for a bag of hot chicken thighs and

the woman in there is getting to know me. She's very attractive. She wears a white hat and coat and she's quite rightly proud of her hot chicken thighs.

She handles them with a long pair of stainless steel tongues, plucking the sizzling thighs from under a glass canopy as I point them out.

'That one please... and that one there.'

Cleanliness is next to Godliness as far as she is concerned and not a single chicken thigh is touched by human hand. Not even by hers, which are scrubbed and gloved, and I haven't the heart to tell her that I buy them for the cats.

I was second in line, behind an old lady in a threadbare coat who was taking forever to pick out a whole cooked chicken from the serried ranks on display. They were lined up as though they were on parade, shortest on the left, tallest on the right.

'How much is that one?'

Too much apparently and she had worked her way through half the regiment before she finished up with the runt of the litter. Still she looked pleased with her choice. He hadn't much meat on him, but he seemed to have a very nice nature.

I felt rather ashamed of myself. There she was with a limited budget, making do, and here I was shopping for the cats. I would have liked to have bought her the biggest one, especially with Christmas just around the corner. But I couldn't think of a way to do it without patronising her. No time for a quick word with the lady in the white coat.

'Give her whatever she wants and I'll pay. Tell her it's only fifty pence.'

So I blew it. I just stood there like an idiot, watching as the puny chicken was slipped into a neat white bag and money changed hands. Then the old lady turned to me and smiled.

'It's for my cat, you know. I buy him one every weekend. He gets ever so excited.'

And so do mine. The minute I step through the front door they home in on me from every corner of the house, noses twitching, taste buds slavering.

The problem is that spoiling them all the year round makes it that bit harder to spoil them at Christmas. It's the same with Aileen and myself. I can remember when a turkey was something special, but now we have a breast joint from Marks and Spencers two or three times a month, with all the trimmings and a couple of bottles of wine. It takes the thrill out of Christmas.

At least the cats can always look forward to the odd surprise. A truck driver in America listens to their adventures on tape as he works his way across the country and every Christmas he sends them a selection of garlic summer sausages in a small wooden box.

It lasts them all through the year. William can't be doing with it, but Thermal and Tigger each have a slice first thing in the morning as part of a calorie controlled diet. It helps keep them fit and healthy for when they go out hunting. They work as a team and their combined garlic breath can stun a field mouse at fifty yards.

Last Christmas an Italian lady sent them a pot of

raspberry jam to share between them.

'I know as when reading your books that they have it on their toast for the breakfast.'

I must have a word with the translator -I think we've got a wire crossed somewhere.

So far this year they have received a couple of catnip mice, a catnip cushion and, from Japan, a pack of playing cards with an astonishing selection of naked women on the back. Perhaps I should have a word with the Japanese translator as well.

One present that always goes down well is a carton of clotted cream that arrives from a cat called Fluffy in Barnstable. This year Fluffy says on the card that he's got a new friend - a half-Persian *kitchen.*

I think Fluffy should have a word with his translator.

38.

DO NOT DISTURB.

My little laptop yawned, drummed its fingers on the desk, and waited. It's only the size of a half-pound box of chocolates, but it's a professional through and through and it can't be doing with amateurs.

'What are we waiting for?'

"Inspiration. I need the cats to do something interesting."

'We could be here forever. Idle little devils.'

It's the same every January - the cats hibernate. This year, Tigger has taken to sleeping in the tablecloth drawer. She buries herself deep among the Spanish lace and Irish linen, only coming up for air when she feels the need to refuel or use the litter tray.

William has curled himself up in my brand new wastepaper basket and I haven't been able to use it for a week. It has a shredder attached and I hate to think what might happen if anyone presses the button. He'd finish up with a tail like an African fly whisk.

At least I can see Thermal. He spends the whole day flat out on my desk, looking for all the world like a Furby whose battery has gone way past its sell-by date.

The laptop can't understand them. He's eager and ready to go 24 hours a day, all the year round, and he's never had a moment's illness in his life.

Maybe he'll get his come-uppance as the year 2000 comes winging in. If the virus strikes, then perhaps he might find out that he's not so tough after all.

In the meantime, I had an article to write for those nice people at Your Cat magazine and I was surrounded by a boring bunch of comatose felines.

"For goodness' sake, do something interesting."

At the sound of my voice, Tigger stirred and hung her chin wearily over the lip of the drawer. She had a lace doily draped over the top of her head and looked like a June bride with a hangover.

'Do you mind? Some of us are trying to sleep.'

Thermal stirred. Or rather he moved a paw about half an inch, one of his ears drooped slightly and both his eyeballs began to revolve as a small burp tried to find the quickest way out.

'What is it – lunch?'

"No it's not. Come on, get up. Do something."

'Burp.'

That wasn't quite what I meant, but at least he twitched once more as the burp made a break for it. William didn't even stir and I was tempted to run something through the shredder, preferably William.

Then the door opened and Little Chap charged in. He'd been missing since Christmas Eve and he had such a tale to tell.

We have long ago stopped thinking of Little Chap as our cat. He comes and goes as he wishes. A couple of weeks is the longest he's ever stayed with us and then he's off. In the early days, we used to go searching for him, putting cards through doors, combing garages and garden sheds. Now we just wait for him to come back, absolutely knackered and starving to death.

Aileen has a theory that he's stationed in the army some-where in Yorkshire and every few weeks he does a runner. I think he's on drugs.

Often I find him out in the courtyard, exhausted and not even able to make it to the back door. But here he was, full of the joys of living and desperate to tell us all about it.

Thermal sprang from the desk and Tigger leapt out of the tablecloth drawer. The wastepaper basket rocked on its heels and William gave a pathetic squeak, so I lifted him out and sat him on the hearthrug.

Little Chap loves an audience. The other three sat entranced as he purred out his story, then all four shot out of the room as though they were on fire.

I followed hard on their heels and there, stuck half in

and half out of the cat flap, was a dead rat. It was huge. It had probably spent a lifetime on anabolic steroids to help with the weightlifting and Little Chap must have dragged it for miles. He was appalled when I quickly disposed of it. 'You bring him a present and he chucks it in the dustbin.'

He stayed out there, wondering how to get the lid off, while the others trooped upstairs with me and dropped off to sleep again.

I think I'll have 40 winks myself. I can't stand all this excitement.

39.

CHIMNEY GAZING.

The woman looked shell-shocked. She stood on my

front doorstep with her hair on end. She had just been

dive-bombed by the little bird who lives in my hanging

basket.

I don't know what sort of bird it is. It's smaller than a

sparrow, with blue flashes. A blue-tit perhaps. I've never

been very good at birds and since this one belts

everywhere at a hundred miles an hour I am not likely to get a close look at him.

It has made a hole the size of a walnut in the side of the basket and pulled all the moss in there. So I presume it must be quite comfy having fashioned itself a settee and two easy chairs with a matching throw and a couple of cushions.

Aileen and I are perfectly safe as it only attacks strangers who ring the bell. We thought we might put up a sign Beware of the Bird, but it seems a lot of trouble when we don't know how long he's going to be with us.

The woman tidied her hair and pulled herself together.

"Do you have a cat?"

"Yes. Three and a half to be exact."

It's just my little joke but she didn't seem to find that at all remarkable. Since Tigger was peeping round the inner door, just head, shoulders and two front paws, she must have assumed that she was the odd half and not Little Chap, who stays with us for just two weeks in every month.

The woman went on.

"Is one of them black?"

"Yes."

"With a white bit under his chin?"

"That's right."

"And does he have a silly expression on his face as though he doesn't quite know what's going on?"

I don't think I've ever heard a better description of William. He looks quite intelligent when he's fast asleep, but then when he wakes up he thinks, "How did I do that?" and the puzzled expression stays with him for the rest of the day.

'You must be talking about William. What's he been up to?'

I invited her in to the hall. Tigger had retreated and was now staring at us round the dining room door, still playing the half cat to perfection.

"He keeps breaking into my house."

For a moment I pictured William wearing a black Balaclava, not realising that the white bit under his chin might give him away. That and the jemmy of course.

"How does he break in?"

"Through the cat flap."

At least he wasn't smashing windows or forcing the door.

"What about your cat?"

"We haven't got one."

She explained that when they first moved in she thought

her husband wanted a cat and he thought she wanted one, and so they had a cat flap put in, all ready. Then they discovered that neither of them liked cats so they didn't get one. Perhaps they should talk more often.

"What does William do?"

"He just walks in, whether we're there or not, and stares up the chimney."

I felt a great surge of affection for William. I had a look round the house before they moved in and it's a great chimney with a cast iron roasting spit and huge hobs on either side.

"He just loves staring up chimneys. It's his hobby."

I suggested she locked the cat flap but she didn't know how to do that and so I walked her home to talk her through it. William was sitting on her path and his face dropped when he saw what we were up to.

I picked him up and tucked him under my arm and then on the way home I had a brilliant idea.

We went round to Bridie's house. She lives just across the back lane and has more chimneys than you've had hot dinners. I explained what had happened and asked her a favour.

"Would you mind if he came and stared up yours?"

She said she wouldn't mind at all and took him into the lounge where he immediately sat on her hearth and peered upwards. She had a log fire going at the time and he was fascinated by all the white bits heading north. The only trouble is that she doesn't have a cat flap, but she says she'll keep an eye open for him and let him in. Perhaps when she gets to know him better we can have a key cut for him. But we'll wait a while yet. It's best not to rush these things.

40.

FAREWELL CHICO.

It's been a sad week. We lost a very good friend in Chico Mendes O'Connell, who passed away in his sleep at the tender age of nine years and a little bit extra that we can't quite work out, because when he was found abandoned in a dustbin on Trinity Street he didn't have his birth certificate with him.

Chico was a small ginger tom-cat of nervous disposition who had been named after the man who saved the rain forests and who lived with Bridie just across the lane.

The combination of being born in Yorkshire and raised by an Irishwoman, who taught him Gaelic from the moment he could walk, had served to give him a rather befuddled air. Being saddled with the name of a Columbian folk hero had proved the final push towards a nervous twitch that would stay with him for life.

Chico was a natural born coward, but he wore it well and nobody around here ever had a bad word to say about him.

For a start he was just about the smallest cat we had ever seen and whilst he was still a kitten the Zybalski's pet rabbit used to beat him up on a regular basis.

The moment the Zybalskis let their pugilistic pet out for its early morning run it would squeeze under the fence and then round to Bridie's to see if Chico was coming out for his early morning duffing up.

It got so that Chico wouldn't even leave his own house unless Bridie went with him and even then he birds used to divebomb him from on high. Even from a hundred feet up something seemed to tell them that here was one of life's victims and they would close in for the kill.

The big turning point in Chico's life came one morning when I popped round to Bridie's to borrow a cup of sugar and some gravy browning. Tigger came with me and as we walked up the path we saw the Zybalski's rabbit playing with what looked like a tennis ball in Bridie's yard.

At least I thought it was a tennis ball, but Tigger is wiser and smarter than I am and she was up that path like a rocket. The rabbit never knew what hit him, but after he'd done a couple of double somersaults and rebounded back off the fence he was beginning to get some sort of an idea.

Tigger chased him all the way in to his hutch and then came back to see how Chico was getting on. It took her some time to persuade him to come out from behind the plantpot, but from that moment on there developed the most loving and lasting of friendships.

Chico became the kitten she had always wanted and Tigger became the mother that Chico had never known. He followed her everywhere, but the first time he followed her home was almost the last.

I was trying very hard not to do any gardening at the time, sitting on the stone mushroom with a cigarette and a cup of coffee, when the pair of them came trooping down the steps.

Chico was so nervous that he asked if he could make use of the facilities, so Tigger pointed out the rockery and then politely turned her back.

He'd just dug himself a small hole and was busily positioning his rear end so that he wouldn't miss when he saw Thermal doing exactly the same thing just the other side of a large white stone.

For a moment the two young cats stared at each other and then Chico was off in a blind panic across the courtyard, only to run straight in to Arthur who was on his way back from having his second breakfast at Gwen's across the road.

Now Arthur was built like a brick outhouse, albeit an outhouse with dodgy back legs and a broken tail, and Chico knew straight away that his time had come. If he couldn't handle a rabbit he would have no chance with a mobile building.

So he was more than surprised when Arthur bent and licked him. Tigger came over to introduce the two of them and Thermal joined them as soon as he could, after he had covered up and tidied over.

From that moment on Chico became the cat who never walked alone. He was never without the company of one or two, or all three of them, the punk with friends in high places and his nine short years were extremely happy and safe.

We will remember him.

41.

IF WISHES WERE KITTENS.

Thermal has taken to sighing a lot I think it's I some sort of mid-life crisis. He sits on my desk for hours on end, watching me work, and every now and then a great big sigh bubbles up from the ends of his paws.

'I should have gone to university'.

He stares at the box of multi-coloured paper clips. He's officer in charge of paper clips and all in all he does a pretty good job in keeping them on their toes, but today

he just dips his paw in among them, stirs them around a

bit and sighs.

'I could have had letters after my name.'

It's getting me down. The last thing you need when you

are desperately trying to finish a new book in time for

the Christmas market is a cat with the monk on,

stretched out on your desk.

'I could have travelled the world.'

"Oh for goodness sake, stop it."

He lies down on a bunch of newspaper cuttings and rests

his chin on my disk drive. And sighs.

'I should have married Marlene Fogarty.'

"She wasn't right for you."

'We would have had kittens by now.'

"Look, I'm trying to write."

This has been going on for at least a week now. The other cats are out playing in the sunshine, mugging mice and violating voles, while Tigger vigorously pursues her various charitable causes. She's found a small kitten who lives just up the lane and has taken on the position of official child-minder. She insists on minding him even though his owners don't want him to be minded and I think they are getting a bit fed up with her.

"She's always here."

They have had the kitten for a couple of months now. He's a cute little thing. They call him Pindrop and they never shut up about him.

"He's so light that when you drop him on the floor, you could hear a pin drop."

Maybe he does need a child-minder if his owners are making a habit of dropping him on the floor. Perhaps

Thermal might like to give Tigger a hand?

I suggested it to him, but he's so wrapped up in himself.

'I blame my dad.'

"You never knew your dad."

'That's what I mean. He was never around.'

I wish he didn't think so much. He's always turning

things over in his mind and it doesn't get you anywhere.

I wish he was more like William. He doesn't think at all.

William lives in his own little world. His memory span

is equivalent to that of a rather dim goldfish. That's why

he can spend hours simply staring up the chimney. He

finds each and every moment of his life so rich and

rewarding, simply because he can never remember what

happened a few seconds ago and so he just sits there,

waiting for it not to happen again.

Little Chap thinks, but only when he's fast asleep. When

he's wide awake his face is as empty as that of a model on a Paris catwalk. But once he drops off to sleep his face takes on a new life.

In his dreams he plays for Manchester United and only the other night he scored a couple of goals at Wembley, the only cat to do so since Puskas captained Hungary against England in November 1953.

I have tried to explain that Puskas wasn't exactly of feline persuasion, but he's not interested in details. In his sleep he climbs mountains and crosses deserts, abseiling and bungee-jumping all the way. He flails about so much that he often falls asleep in the lounge and finishes up in the downstairs toilet. But at least he doesn't sigh.

Thermal had now wrapped himself around the base of my desk lamp. It's brass and it gets ever so warm. He stared at my biro and gave it a desultory flick with his paw. He must have clicked the button on the top because the biro gave a little jump and the ballpoint bit shot out.

A week ago that would have had Thermal in raptures, but today he just sighed.

'I could have won Crufts, you know, if I'd concentrated.'

"That's for dogs."

'Whatever.'

I tried to concentrate on my book. Only one week to go to the deadline. Thermal sighed.

'I blame the government.'

I would like you to look away now, if you wouldn't mind. I'm just about to smash him over the head with my glass ashtray and it won't be a pretty sight

42.

TIGGER'S NEW PAL.

It's been going on for a couple of weeks now and Mrs Rudge has asked me if I'll put a stop to it. Well I've tried, but it's like trying to plait sawdust and I'm getting desperate.

The first I knew about it was when I switched on the kitchen lights early one morning and there was Tigger and a small ginger kitten fast asleep in the laundry basket.

I didn't see the kitten straight away. It was using a pair of my boxer shorts as a makeshift duvet and all I could see was the tip of one ear sticking out through the flap at the front.

'How on earth did this get here, Tigger?'

'I don't know, but can we keep it?'

Well it's not as easy as that. First of all we would have to find out if it belonged to somebody nearby and if that didn't work, advertise him in the local paper. Not that there was all that much to say about him.

'Found in laundry basket - small ginger kitten with a miserable excuse for a tail and a short stumpy leg at each corner.'

But it never came to that. Within the hour Mrs Rudge was standing on the doorstep.

'Sorry to bother you, but you don't happen to have seen a small ginger...'

'Come on in.'

The kitten had been following Tigger around as though it were attached to her rear end by a piece of elastic and they were now watching a children's television programme in the lounge. Tigger doesn't usually watch television, but she must have thought it was the thing to do whenever the kids came round.

Thermal and William weren't too sure about the newcomer. Thermal couldn't decide whether it was a real kitten or some sort of mechanical toy and he was just having a quick sniff to see where you had to put the batteries when Mrs Rudge and I joined them in the lounge.

She was thrilled to see the kitten, far more thrilled than the kitten was to see Mrs Rudge. It snuggled up so close to Tigger that I began to think we might have to operate in order to get it out from underneath her.

For the rest of the day Tigger moped about looking miserable and she was still at when I let her out of the back door around six-thirty that evening.

'He doesn't live far away. You can always visit.'

And she must have taken me at my word because ten minutes later I saw her prancing proudly back up the path with the ginger kitten stuck to her side.

Mrs Rudge wasn't far behind.

'Our Barnaby was just eating his dinner when your cat

came in and took him straight off.'

She bent and scooped up the little kitten, then plonked him in her Sainsbury's carrier bag.

'I'd be gratefully if you would keep her away.'

But that's easier said than done. Since then I have carted little Barnaby back home at least a dozen times. I think Tigger must have a set of skeleton keys and a jemmy hidden away somewhere. She seems to be able to get in to the house at will. If Barnaby isn't over here, then Tigger is over there.

Mrs Rudge has found the pair of them under the bed in the spare room and fast asleep together on the settee.

I think I would be quite pleased if a kitten of mine had found such a loving friend. I mean it's not as though Tigger is some sort of a Madonna looking for a toy boy and there isn't a cat in the neighbourhood who would dare duff him up with Tigger by his side.

This morning Mrs Rudge came banging on the door but for once her kitten wasn't here. But then neither was Tigger. I looked in all the usual places but there was no sign of them.

'Perhaps they've run off to Gretna Green.'

Mrs Rudge didn't think that was at all funny and maybe she was right. She rang me about ten minutes later.

'I've found them. They were fast asleep in my husband's boot.'

I thought 'My God he must have big feet', and then it dawned on me that she was talking about his car.

Mrs Rudge is insistent. She says it's got to stop, but my heart's not in it. I like to see them together.

I'll have another word with Tigger, but I don't know

what the Dickens I'm going to do about Barnaby Rudge.

43.

SKIRTING THE ISSUE.

The lady from the newspaper eased herself back in the

chair and crossed her legs. Or rather I assume she crossed

her legs, she could have had anything hidden underneath

that skirt.

It was a dirndl skirt apparently.

"From *Ghost,*" Claire had whispered as she ushered the

journalist in. 'They cost about a thousand quid.'

If that was true then the material must have cost around about forty pence a metre. I have never seen so much fabric wrapped around a human body. We could have curtained the whole house and still had enough left over for a couple of settees and a scatter cushion.

She uncrossed her legs and this time, amongst the many folds and flounces, I caught a flash of something white. It could have been either a pair of sporty pop socks, or a small white cat who just happened to be passing as she sat down.

She dipped in her bag and pulled out a tape recorder.

'Where are the cats at the moment?'

I told her I wasn't absolutely sure.

'They like to be out and about in this weather.'

All except Thermal of course, who had spent last fortnight

curled up with the Kettley's kids in their wigwam on the back lawn. The kids have adopted him as their official papoose and apparently papooses have to sleep a lot and so the part was right up his street.

Tigger loves sunbathing. She spends every spare moment topping up her ginger bits and since spare moments are all she ever has these days, it's more of a full-time job than a hobby.

Thermal joins her in the courtyard every now and then, but only for a few moments at a time. With his pale colouring you can't be too careful and so he prefers to nod off under the cool shade of the wigwam.

Or under a dirndl skirt perhaps? Right from being a kitten he's always had this talent for crawling under the wrong thing at the wrong time. When he was only a few weeks old he panicked at the sight of two burly delivery men carrying a solid oak bookcase up the drive.

So very sensibly he got out of their way and then very stupidly went and hid under the hall rug. A few minutes later I dragged out this rather flat kitten who had just had two burly delivery men, carrying a solid oak bookcase, walk all over him.

He was a sad sight, all bruised and battered and with a broken wisp of a tail which he dragged pitifully around with him for the next couple of weeks. He was quite proud of the bandage and I must admit he did look rather cute, especially after he had dipped his tail into a leftover dish of chicken korma and turned the white bandage into a rather attractive orange.

Since then he has been locked in the fridge and nailed

up under the floorboards. But loitering with intent is what he does best, burrowing under hearthrugs, duvets and piles of washing.

Once, when we had friends in for a meal, I laid the table ready - with six place settings, sweet smelling candles and a huge vase of flowers, all spread out on a large white cloth. After a pre-dinner drink we all marched in to find that Thermal had provided the finishing touch - a small white, cat-shaped ghost, sitting to attention under the tablecloth, right next to a bottle of red wine that I had left to breathe and which now had breathed its last.

As the journalist went through her list of questions William came in to have a look at her. He was very interested in her skirt which to someone his size must have looked like the big top at a circus, and he sniffed all round the hem and then had a peep underneath. The journalist stiffened.

'I'm sorry, but I am allergic to cats.'

I grabbed hold of William's bum and dragged him out just as he was about to disappear through a little door he'd found in the fabric. A little white head appeared from under the skirt.

'Was that William?'

The journalist went white and so, as cats always do, William jumped up on her knee and tried to make her better. She was still shaking as I helped her aboard the London train and when I got back home I looked around for Thermal, but he was nowhere.

Aileen said he was probably just pulling into Kings Cross Station. I hoped not - it would take weeks for him to find his way out of that skirt, never mind London.

44.

INVASION OF THE UNDIE SNATCHERS.

A couple of friends are staying with us this week, a mother and her teenage daughter, and as I carried their luggage up to the third floor I suggested that they shut their bedroom doors behind them whenever they went out.

Of course they haven't. I warn all of our visitors and not one of them ever takes the slightest bit of notice, and what happens? A small army of cats creep in one by one and go through their underwear, that's what happens.

I once caught Thermal fast asleep on the bed, dozing in one half of a Marks and Spencer's circle stitched bra, while Tigger was all curled up in the other half, doing her nails. Apparently both of my cats are natural 38 D cups and so they fitted in quite nicely.

William is into tights. He once shredded a pair that a guest had hung from the bedpost. I couldn't stop him. In no more than a split second he first swung on them and then climbed up them, like Tarzan scrambling up a vine, and by the time he had finished they were about six foot long and not even fit for straining paint.

The problem is that the guest floor is where the cats normally go for their regular daft half hour. Up there they can be kittens again. Thermal's speciality is tearing around like a dodgem car, upside down under the huge double bed, whilst William jumps in the bath and races round and round until he has re-invented the wall of death.

Tigger sits and watches them disapprovingly, like some prim maiden aunt, until she can stand it no longer, and then she cracks and immediately launches herself into her world famous wardrobe routine.

Over the years she's found out that if she lies on her back and braces her rear legs firmly against the plinth she can yank open the magnetic doors with her front paws.

In the big bedroom we have a line of five built-in wardrobe doors all in a row and she has now perfected the art of door opening to such an extent that she can have the lot of them standing wide open in no time at all. Then she races back down the line and slams them all shut, one after another, by standing up on her hind legs and giving the doors a damn good thump.

I usually leave them to it - it's like bedlam up there for a while, but I know that in half an hour or so they'll all troop downstairs, as good as gold, and then fall fast asleep together in one big hairy lump.

But it's not as simple as that when we have guests staying up there. The half empty suitcases are far too tempting and the cats are in there like a shot. They always seem to go through hers first.

'You see, red knickers. You could tell just by looking at her.'

Then they go through his.

'Well would you believe it. Let's hope he never gets run over.'

I once found Tigger trapped inside a lace body stocking with her claws stuck through the little holes. She hadn't a cat in hells chance of getting out on her own and so I had to go in through that little flap with the poppers and pull her out backwards. God knows what would have happened if our guest had come back unexpectedly. I could have been in *The News of the World.*

At least Tigger leaves the stuff where it is. Thermal drags it out of the case and spreads it all over the room and then I have to creep in and put it all back again.

Since I have absolutely no idea how the case had been packed in the first place it all must look highly suspicious and, maybe I am imagining it, but I do get one or two rather funny looks from our guests.

On the morning after Aileen's last birthday party we were saying goodbye to a couple from Chichester, when one of their suitcases started doing a belly dance on the front step. It was made of soft leather and the sides were pulsating and when we opened it up, Thermal shot out. Another minute and he would have been bound for West Sussex.

Now there's a thought. The mother and daughter are off home tomorrow. I wonder if he would fancy a trip down to Walton on Thames?

I could do with a rest.

45.

ON THE COUCH WITH THERMAL.

He sat in the garden, his bum parked on a lettuce that I don't think I fancy any more. His face was a picture of absolute misery. Thermal is very good at absolute misery - he's practised for years and has it down to a fine art.

'What's wrong?'

He was too choked to speak and so I picked him up and laid him out on the sun lounger.

'Tell me all about it.'

After years of dealing with a whole series of maladjusted cats I now slip in to the role of feline psychiatrist as though moving on well oiled wheels. My small but beautifully marked patient rolled over on to his back.

'Give me a tummy-rub first.'

There can't be many psychiatrists who start off a counselling session by giving their patients a good tummy-rub, but I find it works wonders. It empties the mind and I do it with all the cats except William, who inadvertently emptied his mind when he was about three months old and who has never bothered with it since.

Thermal lay on his back and dribbled slightly. I think he

must have a button tucked away under his fur and when I happen to catch it his mouth flies open and a small fountain is brought into play.

'Now tell me what's wrong.'

He gave a big sigh and the fur on his undercarriage rippled slightly as it worked its way out of his system.

'Is this all there is to life?'

I wasn't quite sure what he meant by *all this*. He seems to have a pretty eventful life as far as I can see. There's his day job where he sits on my desk and looks after my paperclips. He takes that very seriously, and then first thing every morning he also has his paper round. He only does our house and the house next door and I must admit, because he happens to be physically ill equipped for pushing newspapers through letter boxes, his role is severely restricted to sniffing each and every paper to see if the paper lad's got it right - but it is essential work and he's very thorough.

Then there's his role as chief irritant to Mrs Cartwright's poodle Buffy. He chased Buffy up a tree last week. It's only a small tree that happens to grow at right angles to the ground and so the result wasn't quite as spectacular as it might sound, but it livened up no end when the resident thrush chased Buffy back down again and then both bird and cat joined forces and cornered the poodle by the water butt near Mrs Cartwright's french windows.

Sometimes I feel sorry for Buffy, but what can he expect if he will go poncing about in a tartan jacket?

I finished off the tummy-rub up under Thermal's chin and he gave a good long gulp and another short dribble.

'And the kids never ring.'

'You haven't got any kids.'

And I know that for a fact. He was nothing but a kid himself when I took him to the vet to have him seen to. Marlene from the pub had started fluttering her eyes at him and everyone around here knows exactly what Marlene is up to.

She's in that taproom from eleven o'clock in the morning until eleven o'clock at night and then she's off on the prowl until the early hours. She's no better than she ought to be - a sad case of secondary drinking.

Thermal sighed once more - a big deep sigh, that came right up from his boots, and for a few moments it seemed as though he would never breathe in again.

'And I'm putting on weight.'

'It suits you.'

'Does it really?'

'Yes. You were too thin before. You're just rounded off nicely now.'

I think he quite liked the idea of being nicely rounded off and he seemed to perk up a little, but then he slumped back down on the sun lounger, his fat little thighs splayed out, looking for all the world as though he had borrowed them for the day from a corn-fed chicken.

'I might as well end it all.'

'Tell you what.'

'What?'

'I've got a dozen prawns in the fridge.'

He was on all fours and quivering slightly.

'They'll go off if someone doesn't eat them soon.' He was

waiting for me by the kitchen door.

'And we won't tell the others.'

He feels much better now. I don't know why they make so

much fuss about psychiatry. It's a doddle.

46.

WHO WERE YOU WITH LAST NIGHT?

The phone rang. I'm still not used to it. The old phone sort of apologised every time it rang.

'Look I hate to bother you, but there's someone on the other end who insists on a quick word. I told them you were busy but...'

And then the poor old thing would trail off until I assured him that he was only doing his job and I really didn't mind, but eventually he stopped ringing altogether and so I pensioned him off to the back bedroom where he only has to deal with outgoing calls. He loves it up there and has a smile on his face once more. The new phone has no such inhibitions.

'Hey you. Get your butt over here and answer this call.'

I am going to have to show him who's the boss around here, but then I have a feeling he knows that already.

Mrs Bramley was on the end of a much nicer phone altogether and she was worried about Tigger.

'I thought you should know. She's sitting in the back lane talking to a big black dog.'

Now a few weeks ago I would have been worried to death at the news and immediately rushed out to see if I could snatch Tigger from the jaws of death.

But the big black dog is called Eamonn and he's as soft as grease. He spends his days strolling round the village, popping in to the shops and attempting to give drivers a heart attack.

He stands on the kerb, looks first right and then left and then right again before strolling across the road whether there is anything coming or not. Whenever we hear the smell of burning rubber and the squeal of brakes we know that Eamonn is off on his rounds once more.

Tigger had always given him a wide birth until about a month ago when the paperboy left the gate open and Eamonn strolled in to have a look around.

Now it's not nice when you are a small cat, no longer in the first flush of youth, with a touch of rheumatism playing silly devils in your back legs and you are having a quiet snooze on your favourite paving stone when all of a sudden a big black dog creeps up on you in your own yard and has a good long sniff at your bottom.

Tigger was furious and when she is furious she is a sight to behold. One thing I love about cats is their bravery under fire. As a contest it was rather like you or me having a scrap with an articulated lorry, but to hell with that. She was on her feet in a flash and in two seconds flat she had given Eamonn a couple of right hooks, a half a dozen straight lefts and an almighty wallop on the nose. One of the things I love about Eamonn is his basic decency. He just sat there and took it like a man. He knew he was in the wrong, butting in like that, and so he waited until Tigger had run out of steam and then with his tail scything happily from side to side, he ambled out through the back gate.

It was a week or so before they met again. Eamonn and I

walked back from the shops together and Tigger was waiting for me on the low wall at the end of the lane.

I had bought my canine friend a bone from the butchers and he was carrying it in his mouth. Tigger jumped down from the wall and Eamonn went over to say hello. He dropped his bone at her feet.

'You can have a lick if you want.'

She gave it a good sniff instead. As a snack it was a bit rough and ready as far as she was concerned. She prefers her meat already cut up into bite sized morsels, smothered in a piquant sauce.

'Very pleasant.'

'Thank you.'

We walked the rest of the way together. Me in the middle, with a cat on one side and a dog with a big bone on the other. I felt as though I was in one of those Disney movies where we have to battle our way home against all the odds, just the three of us and a sixty piece orchestra. So I don't have to worry any more. As we parted Eamonn had another quick sniff at Tigger's bottom and she thumped him hard round the ear. It must be love.

47.

PSSST... FANCY A BIT OF WHEELER-DEALING?

I sit in my office and watch them on close-circuit television as they stroll up the path towards the front door. A whole host of visiting cats, some on the make, some on the cadge and some on tenterhooks as they sniff here and there, picking up the scent of the residents.

We get all sorts. Every month or so a large black tom turns in through the gate. We call him Herbert and I am sure he lives with a travelling family. He wears his fur pulled down over one eye and always seems to have a rather shady deal in the offing.

This morning Thermal met him by the hydrangea bush and although I couldn't hear the conversation I can guess how it went.

'Morning squire. I've got some contract carpeting in the van. Surplus to requirements. Do you a good deal.'

They padded off together to have a look, even though I know for a fact that Thermal doesn't have two ha'pennies to rub together.

Whilst they were gone a friend of Tigger's came to visit. Marlene is part of a large family who live over the other side of the park, two other cats and four dogs and the lack of privacy seems to be wearing her down.

'I've just about had enough.'

Tigger took her round the back where they could sit on the bench together, away from William's ever open ears.

'I try, I really do, but kittens these days, they're not brought up the way we were. They don't have the same standards. And those dogs. They mean well and there's no harm in them, but they're forever barking their heads off and when you boil it all down they've said nothing.'

Tigger nodded. She's a good listener. She's practised for years on Thermal.

William in the meantime had drifted off to stare down his drain. He saw a mouse down there about a year ago and ever since he's put in an eight hour day, week in week out, waiting to see another one.

He has hinted from time to time that it might be a good idea if I sent him off with a packed lunch so that he wouldn't have to break off when the hunger pains begin to strike, but I believe in having the whole family round the table as often as possible and I know the thin end of a wedge when I see one.

As it turned out I had more than the family round the table that evening. Marlene joined us, not in a hurry to be off home.

'I turns my stomach the way those dogs eat. There's food flying everywhere.'

Then Thermal gave Herbert a hefty push and in he tumbled through the back door and so I went off in search of more saucers.

Herbert immediately spotted an opportunity and his eyes lit up.

'I could do you a good deal on some saucers. They're

unbreakable. Even when you throw wooden balls at

them.'

I declined his kind offer and gave him a soup bowl filled

to the brim with chunks of this and chunks of that. From

past experience I've learned that Herbert isn't the most

discerning of eaters.

I once saw him polish off a bowl of dog food that had

been sitting out on our neighbour's back doorstep for a

fortnight while the family were up in the Lake District.

He almost had to use a hammer and chisel to get through

the crust, but he made it and polished it off and then

licked his lips afterwards.

'Very nice. Reminds me of my mother's cooking.'

So after he had licked his soup bowl clean he went to

work on Marlene's leftovers before falling fast asleep,

with his head resting on my foot. Wheeling and dealing must be a very tiring business. I didn't like to disturb him and so Aileen and I worked on the crossword for a while. Marlene had to be off and Tigger went with her as far as the park.

William was anxious to get back to his drain and quietly slipped out through the catflap while Thermal went looking in the dining room for a cheese and onion crisp he'd hidden behind the wine rack. An hour later Herbert was still fast asleep, his head still resting lightly on my foot, which by now had also nodded off and was under attack by a whole battalion of pins and needles. I lifted his head, took my foot away and then stuffed the empty shoe back under his cheek, before limping off to help Thermal find his crisp. It doesn't do to spoil them, does it?

48.

THAT'S ALL FOLKS.

I watched as Tigger eased herself gingerly out of her basket. Her arthritis has been giving her a lot of trouble recently and so before she tried to stand up she had a quiet word with each of her legs in turn, explaining in great detail exactly what was required of them.

The front legs seemed to take it in alright, but her back legs appear to have gone rather deaf of late and they find working as a team somewhat difficult. The left one staggered slightly and the right one had to do a sort of soft shoe shuffle in order to keep the boss upright.

'Watch out – we'll have her over.'

From the basket she had to make her way across the central heating boiler, from where she had to jump down on to a small stool, prior to making her final descent and the safety of the cellar floor. She teetered on the edge of the boiler, staring down at the stool for a while as she worked out the distance and the angles - and then, when she had done her sums and checked them over a couple of times, she began to relay the information to both sets of legs.

'Can you speak up please - we can't hear you at the back.'

I decided to save her the trouble so I reached over and picked her up, plonking her down on the bit of old carpet that we pinched out of Aileen's mother's downstairs toilet while she was away on holiday.

Tigger's back legs gave me a shy smile as they passed me on the way down.

'Thank you very much - we could have managed you know.'

'Of course you could.'

'We're just feeling a bit stiff this morning.'

'I quite understand.'

I have also been keeping an eye on Thermal lately and that hasn't proved as difficult as it would have done in times gone by. Whereas he used to spend his days outside in the fresh air, sniffing at each and every flower in the garden, or leaping to catch birds a hundred feet above his head, before hurrying off to annoy next door's Alsatian, he now sleeps all day on the bench in the corner of the courtyard.

It's the same indoors. The paper clips on my desk never had a spare moment to themselves whenever Thermal was about, he was always rounding them up, sorting them out and giving them a jolly good talking to.

'For goodness sake get a grip on yourselves.'

Spiders would tiptoe past my office door, knowing that one false move would have Thermal out there and in karate mode, his right front paw cocked, a lethal weapon.

'Ha! Grasshopper!'

'I'm a spider actually.'

Whatever, in the old days they would always finish up as a

bunch of very flat spiders indeed. But now both they and the paperclips are living the life of Riley, with Thermal spending hour after hour fast asleep under the brass lamp on my desk.

William hasn't changed all that much in the time he has been with us. When he first arrived he was three and a half years old, going on ninety-five. He spends his summer days staring down drains looking for mice, and the whole of the winter months staring up the chimney for hours on end, looking for goodness knows what. He has always been old before his time.

I called all three of them together for a conference.

'Look chaps I've been thinking.'

They stared at one another in amazement. They had never realised that I did anything as dangerous as thinking.

'We're none of us getting any younger, are we?

They could hardly argue with that - mainly because they had all fallen fast asleep again.

The problem is that appearing every month in "Your Cat" magazine for the past four years has taken it out of them. Show business is a long hard grind and they are not kittens any more. They are worn out and feeling both their age and the pressure of being in the public glare.

'Come on; wake up.'

Three pairs of eyes stared up at me briefly and then six little eyelids began to slide down once more, obeying the law of gravity.

So they are going to retire for the time being. Like worn out old horses I shall let them kick their heels up in the paddock. Thermal opened just the one eye.

'Will we still get our pocket money?'

'Of course you will.'

'That's alright then.'

49.

LIFE BELOW STAIRS.

I pushed open the cellar door with some trepidation. I never know who's going to be in residence first thing in the morning and so I took Tigger down with me - she'd sort out any troublemakers. With all this wet weather and Christmas fast approaching we get all manner of feline flotsam stretched out in the cat baskets.

There was a big black tom on the boiler. I'd seen him before - selling *The Big Issue* down by the market and I tried to remember whether I'd bought one or not. He gave me the sort of look that suggested I hadn't and so I gave him a wide birth as I juggled with the empty bowls and the various tins of Whiskas.

Tigger had velcroed herself to my ankle. In feline body language it tells the newcomers not to worry about me.

'It's alright - he's as soft as grease.'

There were a couple I hadn't seen before, the big black tom and a half grown kitten-cat that must have started out a pristine white when he was living at home with his mother.

He'd let himself go somewhat and his coat had turned a mucky grey - only his snowy-white roots giving any hint that there might be just a touch of upper-class breeding in there somewhere. A bit like the students down at the university.

A pair of regulars squatted on the piano stool. They arrived as a team about a fortnight ago, wet and weary and very, very ginger. I don't think they've been out through the cat-flap since the day they arrived, except to use the outside toilet under the hedge.

I serve them breakfast, lunch and dinner, but they have yet to make eye contact with me. Unlike the black tom who glared at me like a boxer weighing up an opponent.

I had just filled four bowls to overflowing when Little Chap tumbled in through the cat flap. He never manages to make a proper job of it. The other cats leap in and out as though they are practising for the Badminton horse trials. Little Chap does his own version of the Fosbury flop and more often than not, lands flat on his bum.

He staggered upstairs with Tigger and me. As he

accompanied us through the inner door from the cellar there was a collective snort behind us.

'It's alright for some.'

Little Chap stays at home most of the time nowadays, but every now and then the wanderlust becomes too much for him and he takes off for a day or two - to an unknown place where somebody takes him gently by the front paws and drags him through a hedge backwards.

I dried him off with a towel and then did the same for Thermal. He wasn't the slightest bit damp, he hadn't been out of the house for a week, but he demands equal time - he says it's in his contract.

Tigger jumped up and settled down for a nap on the sheepskin saddle that hangs from the radiator. She spends most of her day in there. I bought three of them last

Christmas and two of them have been full of cats ever since.

Little Chap jumped up on to his, fell off and tried again - he insists on taking a run at it and he usually misses the first time.

Thermal stood on his back legs, balancing like a short-sighted meerkat, and peered down at his sheepskin bed. He keeps all his toys and bits and pieces in there - his furry mouse, a once bright red smartie that is now a pale pink and a shadow of its former self, an empty cotton reel, a cotton wool bud - there are lots more but I haven't the time.

He checked that they were all there, tapped his mouse fondly, and then settled down to sleep on the carpet underneath.

Within minutes they were all out like a light. When people ask me why I don't write so much about my cats these days - there's the answer.

They are getting on in years. Their daily routine is to sleep for a good eighteen hours and then have six hours rest. During the summer months those six hours are spent sprawled on my desk, the odd back leg draped across my keyboard.

'Come on you lot - you're boring.'

Tigger half opens a sleepy eye and inquires of Thermal.

'Is he talking about us?'

'No - he wouldn't dare.'

I think Aileen and I might spend Christmas in the cellar, watching the newcomers opening their presents.

At least there might be a punch-up.

50.

TIGGER IS SEVENTEEN NOW...

Tigger doesn't seem to wash herself anymore and yet her fur looks as though it has just come back from the cleaners. I mentioned it to Aileen at breakfast the other morning. She thought about it for a moment or so.

'She probably has someone in.'

That must be what it is. That and the fact that nowadays neither of the cats ever go anywhere, they haven't been out of the house since last October.

We have bought them each one of those small oil-filled radiators that come up to just below my knee, but which are head high to the average cat. They get a top to toe roasting and in front of each radiator there is a very small sheepskin rug, each one stylishly fashioned from a very small sheep. There they sleep side by side, sometimes for twenty-one hours a day. A visitor once looked at them in disgust.

'Idle devils.'

But of course they're not. The author Val Schaffner once said that cats don't just sleep, they prowl the dream landscape together and have adventures that we can never imagine.

But if people think they are bone idle then so much the better. They reason that if humans only knew of the amazing talents the average cat has at his command, then they would make them work for a living.

Tigger is seventeen years old now and the dreaded arthritis has tied her muscles into twisted knots. Once she would bound up the stairs to my office without ever seeming to touch the carpet, but lately I have been wondering if I could persuade Stannah to bring out a range of very small stair lifts.

She only has the one tooth which means that I have to be very selective when filling her bowl. I have nothing against Tigger's tooth, but then neither has Tigger and so pâtés are the order of the day, along with finely chopped tuna, corned beef and garlic sausage.

The cats always arrive at the kitchen table buttoned up together like Siamese twins, but then once under cover of the table they separate, Thermal banging his flank hard against Aileen's ankle, Tigger against mine.

'We're here.'

And then, rejoined at the hip, they sit staring intently at the fridge door, believing that through the power of their joint personalities they can persuade the door to swing wide open. The fact that this has never actually happened in the last sixteen years hasn't served to dull their belief, but then their rumbling stomachs tell them that there's always a next time and they decide to cut corners by standing on their hind legs and clawing their way in through the wooden panel on the fridge door.

'No.'

This order, barked out by the fearsome man of the house is always obeyed immediately and they stop short and sit and stare again in unison until Tigger, who simply can't bear to be told what to do, raises one limp paw and with her claws completely withdrawn taps gently just once against the door.

'I'm not having him talking to me like that.'

'You do right.'

Thermal still likes to think of himself as a man about town, but really he's now just a man about the sheepskin rug. The other day I carried him up to the office and sat him on my desk, where he once worked as officer in charge of paper clips.

In Thermal's time the paper clips never had a minute to

themselves. He rounded up the strays and saw to it that they were kept constantly on the move, they were lean, mean and ready for action. Now they just lie there, flabby and out of condition.

But he wasn't interested. It was three o'clock in the afternoon and well after the time for his eight-hour post luncheon nap. So I took him back downstairs where he immediately collapsed on to his very small rug.

I sat on the carpet and watched them for a while. Tigger completely relaxed, but still every inch a lady with her tilted chin and her paws drawn up at half mast, her arthritis forgotten for the moment. Thermal the tiny kitten I brought into the house on a shovel some sixteen years ago, stretched out untidily and snoring his head off, legs all over the place as though he wasn't quite sure they were his. And I thought of all the joy and companionship, the heartaches and worries they brought with them when they decided all that time ago that this was where they wanted to be and I hugged myself with pleasure.

I wouldn't have missed a moment of it.

The End

About Deric Longden

Deric Longden passed away in June 2013. He was born in Chesterfield in 1936 and married Diana Hill in 1957. They had two children, Sally and Nick. After various jobs he took over a small factory making women's lingerie, but began writing and broadcasting in the 1970s and before long he was writing regularly for programmes like 'Does He Take Sugar?' and 'Woman's Hour'. Most of his work was based on his own experience. The demands made on him by Diana's illness, subsequently believed to be a form of ME, forced him to sell the factory, and since then he devoted himself to full-time writing, broadcasting, lecturing and after-dinner speaking.

Diana's Story, published in 1989, some years after Diana's death, was a bestseller. The book hit the Sunday Times best seller list straight away, won the NCR book award. It was followed by Lost for Words, The Cat Who Came in from the Cold, I'm a Stranger Here Myself, Enough to Make a Cat Laugh and A Play On Words. Deric Longden's first two books were adapted for television under the titles Wide-Eyed and Legless, and an adaptation of Lost for Words. Both were nominated for multiple BAFTAs and Lost For Words, screened in January 1999, attracting an audience of more than 12 million viewers and won the Emmy for Best Foreign Drama and a BAFTA for Dame Thora Hird as best actress.

He married the writer Aileen Armitage in 1990 and they lived together in Huddersfield. Aileen and he were jointly were awarded honorary Doctor of Literature from Huddersfield University in 2004 and Deric a honorary Master of Letters from Derby University in 2006.

ALSO AVAILABLE AS BOTH KINDLE EBOOKS AND IN PRINT BY DERIC LONGDEN

LOST FOR WORDS

DIANA'S STORY

I'M A STRANGER HERE MYSELF

THE CAT WHO CAME IN FROM THE COLD

ENOUGH TO MAKE A CAT LAUGH
LAUGH

A PLAY ON WORDS

AVAILABLE AS KINDLE EBOOKS BY DERIC LONGDEN

RADIO TIMES TAKE 1

RADIO TIMES TAKE 2

RADIO TIMES TAKE 3

RADIO TIMES TAKE 4

THIS SPORTING LIFE

Printed in Great Britain
by Amazon

34555427R00185